# DIFFERENTIAL FERTILITY
# IN CENTRAL INDIA

# Differential Fertility in Central India

EDWIN D. DRIVER

PRINCETON UNIVERSITY PRESS
PRINCETON, NEW JERSEY, 1963

Publication of this book has been aided by the
Population Council, Inc., and by the
Ford Foundation program to support publication,
through university presses, of work in the
humanities and social sciences.

Printed in the United States of America

*To my family:*
*Aloo, Shernaz, Shanta, and Cyrus*

# Preface

THE purpose of this volume is to provide an accurate description of population dynamics in Central India. It presents the patterns of fertility and mortality prevailing among various social strata and seeks to isolate the physical and cultural factors which account for fertility differentials. It also delineates the attitudes of couples toward birth control techniques and family limitation.

The need for studies of this kind was succinctly stated in 1957 in papers presented at the Inaugural Conference of the United Nations Demographic Training and Research Centre, Bombay. It was stated again in 1961 by scholars and governmental officials attending the eleventh conference of the Food and Agricultural Organization. We hope that our findings will prove to be of value to economic planners, demographers, and other persons who are greatly interested in population growth in India.

The completion of this study was made possible by the assistance and support of many persons and organizations. I wish to acknowledge my gratitude to the following students of Nagpur University who participated in the study as interviewers: Misses R. D. Chakradeo, B. Das, V. Desai, S. Parate, S. Raghavan, V. Singh, and A. D. Variava; Mrs. S. Bhide; and Messrs. S. C. Behar, R. T. Burznik, L. R. Choudhary, S. S. Chouganjhar, W. V. Damke, S. W. Deshpande, D. N. Dhanagare, K. K. Dubey, P. Ferráo, M. M. Golpelwar, S. D. Iyer, M. K. Janbaz, C. W. Lakhe, S. S. Lele, P. Madura, A. G. Moghe, N. Nayudu, P. D. Pathak, R. K. Pillai, S. R. Pinjarkar, S. Rao, R. S. Sapre, B. B. Shaligam, N. R. Siddqui, N. K. Sonak, R. N. Swamy, and M. Vermgopolam. A special debt is owed Mr. Mathew Verghese and Mrs. Edwin D. Driver who assisted in training the interviewers, supervising the field work, and coding the interview material. Lastly, I wish to express my gratitude for the financial support rendered by the U.S. Educational Foundation in India, the Population Council, Inc., and the Research Council of the University of Massachusetts.

EDWIN D. DRIVER

vii

# Contents

# Tables

# Figures

# DIFFERENTIAL FERTILITY IN CENTRAL INDIA

# Introduction

THE future pattern of population growth in India will have a decisive bearing on whether the several economic and social objectives set forth in the Five-Year Plans are achieved. For more than a half-century a high mortality rate has operated to almost counterbalance a high and stable fertility rate, thus preventing a rapid increase in population size. In the future, however, the past influence of mortality is expected to be considerably less. Deaths due to malnutrition, famines, and gastro-intestinal ailments are being decreased through improved agricultural production and distribution and the purification of water supplies. In addition, the Government of India and the World Health Organization have launched national programs of medical care and preventive medicine which, on the basis of recent surveys, appear effective in lowering the incidence of smallpox, cholera, plague, malaria, filariasis, tuberculosis, and venereal diseases. The success of the National Malaria Campaign is indicated by the following reductions between 1953 and 1956 in the spleen rate in various states: 56 to 19 in Bihar; 40 to 14 in Madhya Pradesh; 34 to 18 in Orissa; and 20 to 7 in West Bengal.[1] By 1961, the B.C.G. program was expected to protect the majority of tuberculin negatives under 20 years of age.[2] Control over these and other primary causes of death implies a rapid drop in the mortality rate[3] and, on the basis of evidence gathered during the filariasis campaign, a decrease in the incidence of sterility in the population.

[1] C. Chandrasekharan, "India's Population Problem," Unpublished Paper presented at the Inaugural Conference of the Demographic Teaching and Research Centre, Bombay, on November 5, 1957, p. 5.

[2] *Ibid.*

[3] It is, of course, possible that the transformations in the natural and material environment resulting from economic development will give rise to new and major causes of disability and death. Limited evidence of this occurrence is provided by the United Nations Secretariat, Bureau of Social Affairs, *International Survey of Programmes of Social Development*, New York: United Nations, 1959, pp. 14–15, 27.

TABLE 1

Average Annual Births, Deaths, and Natural Increase per 1000 Population, India, 1881 to 1961*

| Decade | Births | Deaths | Natural Increase |
|--------|--------|--------|------------------|
| 1881–1891 | 48.9 | 41.3 | 7.6 |
| 1891–1901 | 45.8 | 44.4 | 1.4 |
| 1901–1911 | 49.2 | 42.6 | 6.6 |
| 1911–1921 | 48.1 | 47.2 | 0.9 |
| 1921–1931 | 46.4 | 36.3 | 10.1 |
| 1931–1941 | 45.2 | 31.2 | 14.0 |
| 1941–1951 | 43.1 | 30.9 | 12.2 |
| 1951–1961 | 40.0 | 21.7 | 18.3 |

* The rates for the decades 1881–1891 to 1931–1941 are provided by Kingsley Davis, *The Population of India and Pakistan*, Princeton: Princeton University Press, 1951, p. 85. The rates for the decade 1941–1951 are provided by the Office of Population Research, Princeton, and presented in C. Chandrasekharan, "India's Population Problem," Unpublished Paper presented at the Inaugural Conference of the Demographic Teaching and Research Centre, Bombay, on November 5, 1957, p. 3.

The rates for the decade 1951–1961 are presented in the *Demographic Yearbook*, 1960, New York: United Nations, 1960, pp. 483 and 505. They were obtained from results of the 7th and 14th rounds of the National Sample Survey, Government of India, and they are for the rural areas only. The 7th round in 1953 provides a birth rate of 40.9 and a death rate of 24.0 whereas the 14th round in 1958 provides a birth rate of 39.1 and a death rate of 19.4. The rates for 1951–1961 given in the table are averages of the two rounds.

The potential effect of declining mortality on population growth and economic development in India is vividly described by Coale and Hoover.[4] Their estimates, which assume an increase in the average expectation of life at birth from 32 years in 1951 to 52 years in 1986, show a population of 775 millions by 1986 if no change occurs in the current fertility rate. But, if it is assumed that a 50 per cent reduction in fertility occurs in linear fashion between 1956–1981 or between 1966–1981, then the figures would be 589 and 634 millions, respectively.[5] The gain in per capita income, 1986 over 1956, would be 38 per cent if fertility did not decline and 95 per cent, the goal of India, if the decline began in 1956.[6]

[4] A. J. Coale and E. M. Hoover, *Population Growth and Economic Development in Low-Income Countries*, Princeton: Princeton University Press, 1958.
[5] *Ibid.*, pp. 34–37.
[6] *Ibid.*, p. 272.

4

In this context, the future course of fertility has great importance. In the opinion of many demographers, a significant decline in fertility requires quick acceptance by the public of the birth control programs which have been introduced by the Government of India and voluntary associations. In the absence of deliberate controls, they argue,

TABLE 2

Estimates of India's Population (in millions) between 1961 and 1981*

| Source | 1961** | 1971 | 1976 | 1981 |
| --- | --- | --- | --- | --- |
| Census of India, 1951, Part I-A, Report | 407 | 464 | — | 529 |
| Planning Commission, India, Second Five-Year Plan | 401 | 459 | 494 | 529 |
| Office of Population Research, Princeton | | | | |
|   Fertility declining by 50%—1956 to 1981 | 420 | 494 | 531 | 562 |
|   Fertility unchanged | 424 | 532 | 601 | 682 |

* SOURCE: A. J. Coale and E. M. Hoover, *Population Growth and Economic Development in Low-Income Countries*, Princeton: Princeton University Press, 1958, p. 42.

** According to a preliminary count of the 1961 census, India's population grew from 361 millions in 1951 to 438 millions in 1961, an increase of 21.5 per cent. Source: *New York Times*, April 2, 1961, p. 9.

Comparison of the various estimates for 1961 with this official, preliminary count would lead one to conclude that population has grown more rapidly than was expected if it were not for the fact that (1) the estimates are minimal rather than maximal figures and (2) the actual size of population in 1951 was probably greater than 361 millions, the figure that was used in making the estimates for 1961 and subsequent years. With regard to the 1951 census count of 361 millions, the Census Commissioner observes that "for every thousand persons included in the census count, eleven other persons were probably omitted." Source: Census of India, 1951, Part I-A, *Report*, Delhi: Manager of Publications, 1953, p. 2.

change should not be expected since the rate of fertility has remained constant over the past fifty years. One factor which might invalidate this argument is the fact that India's social structure which was relatively static during this period is not expected to remain so. It is therefore possible, but improbable in the short run, that fertility patterns, even in the absence of deliberate controls, will be altered by the numerous changes in social structure and social norms produced by the Five-Year Plans and new governmental policies.

These changes include, among others, modification in the proportions of persons who are educated, living in urban areas, owning land, and employed in various occupations. According to the Planning Commission, the "Second Plan will ... begin for the first time in fifty years, barring the two war periods, to increase the proportion of persons employed outside of agriculture and it will lay the foundation in industry and elsewhere which will expand employment over the future."[7] The present 70:30 ratio of agricultural to nonagricultural employment will probably be reduced to 60:40 by 1975–1976.[8] The occupations whose representation in the total labor force is expected to increase most include: semi-skilled and skilled workers; engineers, doctors and nurses; rural extension workers; and managerial and administrative personnel.[9] An illustration of the possible extent of their increase is provided by the Second Five-Year Plan, which runs from 1956 to 1961: one goal is 750,000 *new* semi-skilled and skilled industrial workers by 1961, which number is almost equal to the total (825,000) workers of this kind found in India in 1956.[10] As indicated previously, income levels are also expected to change, providing a reduction in the proportion of persons now found in the low income groups. The proportions of the population who are landless and who have large land holdings may be reduced by various land reform measures. Greater opportunities for primary and secondary schooling and the adult literacy campaign are expected to alter the distribution of persons in various educational categories.

## GENERAL PURPOSE OF THIS STUDY

The general purpose of this study is to determine whether there is any basis for assuming a change in fertility in Central India as a consequence of changes in the proportions of persons currently found in various residential, religious, caste, occupational, income, land ownership, and educational groups. As we have partly indicated, the

[7] Government of India, Planning Commission, *The New India: Progress Through Democracy*, New York: Macmillan, 1958, p. 99.

[8] Government of India, Planning Commission, *Second Five-Year Plan*, Delhi: Manager of Publications, 1956, pp. 12–14.

[9] Government of India, Planning Commission, *The New India: Progress Through Democracy*, pp. 102–110.

[10] *Ibid.*

Five-Year Plans will provide the opportunity for and, if they are to be successful, will necessitate changes in residential, economic and educational patterns. Shifts in religious membership, on the other hand, are a matter of personal choice and may occur at any time. These shifts, especially from Hinduism to other religions, may lead individuals or subgroups to disclaim caste affiliation. A change in caste identity may, however, occur in quite another manner. Today a special commission is authorized by the Government of India to inquire periodically into the economic and educational levels of subcastes and decide whether or not they should be included in or excluded from the Backward Castes and Scheduled Castes.

There are two conditions which must exist before one can reasonably assume that the general fertility rate will be affected by the above-mentioned changes in social structure. First, it must be demonstrated that fertility varies among groups which are currently differentiated in social status. Secondly, it is necessary to demonstrate that the fertility of persons who shift from one status to another resembles that of the group in which they gain membership. This study, which is based on a sample survey conducted in Central India, is limited to the first consideration. The smallness of our sample and the insignificant amount of past and present change in social status prevents our giving attention to the second consideration. The specific objectives and methodology of this study will be indicated after a review of studies of differential fertility which have been completed in other parts of India.

## PREVIOUS STUDIES OF DIFFERENTIAL FERTILITY

Several investigators provide reports of fertility patterns among groups differentiated according to either residence, religion, caste, economic status, or education.

### RESIDENCE, RELIGION, AND CASTE

On the basis of these studies, which were conducted in selected areas of India, fertility is not related to urban or rural residence. The survey of Poona District by the Gokhale Institute found that the number of births per 1000 married women is 6456 in the city and 6408 in the non-city areas.[11] In three neighboring districts surveyed by the Institute, rural women in two of them had slightly higher gross reproductive and maternal net reproductive rates than the urban women. In the other district, the rural women had a slightly higher gross net reproductive rate but a somewhat lower maternal net reproductive rate.[12] In other regions of India, the urban-rural differences are likewise insignificant. A special report of the 1951 Census of India provides the following averages for urban and rural women, respectively, in various regions who were still married at age 45 or over: 6.4 and 6.6 in Travancore-Cochin; 6.3 and 6.1 in Eastern Madhya Pradesh; 6.4 and 6.6 in other regions of Madhya Pradesh; and 6.7 and 6.2 in other regions of India.[13] The National Sample Survey by comparing the fertility of urban and rural couples in various parts of India after 2, 7, 12, and 22 years of marriage concludes that there is no difference between them, except that part arising out of premature marriages in the rural sector.[14]

Less attention has been given to fertility rates among religious and caste groups. In Poona District, the observed rates in the city are higher for Hindus and Jains than for Muslims, Christians, and other non-Hindus. Within the Hindu group, Brahmins have lower rates than the Backward Castes and Other Castes.[15] But, in the non-city area of Poona District, neither religious nor caste affiliation bears a relation to fertility.[16] Striking differences among castes in fertility are also absent in neighboring districts and other regions of India.[17]

[11] V. M. Dandekar and K. Dandekar, *Survey of Fertility and Mortality in Poona District*, Poona: Gokhale Institute of Politics and Economics, Publication No. 27, 1953, p. 96.

[12] N. V. Sovani and K. Dandekar, *Fertility Survey of Nasik, Kolaba, and Satara (North) Districts*, Poona: Gokhale Institute of Politics and Economics, Publication No. 31, 1955, pp. 71, 158.

[13] A. J. Coale and E. M. Hoover, *op. cit.*, pp. 47–48.

[14] A. D. Gupta, R. K. Sen, M. Majumdar and S. N. Mitra, *The National Sample Survey, No. 7: Couple Fertility*, New Delhi: Department of Economic Affairs, Ministry of Finance: Government of India, 1955, p. 38.

[15] V. M. Dandekar and K. Dandekar, *op. cit.*, p. 63.

[16] *Ibid.*, pp. 96, 101.

[17] A. D. Gupta (*et al*), *op. cit.*, p. 41.

*ECONOMIC STATUS*

When previous studies of economic status and fertility are juxtaposed, one obtains an unclear picture of the relation between these two variables. The United Nations-Government of India Survey of Mysore, using type of dwelling as an index of the economic status of the family, found a positive association between completed fertility (that of women 45 years of age or over) and upper status. Rural women living in huts had 4.4 live births, whereas those living in "mudhouses with thatched roof" had 4.5 live births and those living in still better houses had 5.0 live births.[18] Similarly, the wives of agricultural laborers had 4.0 live births, while those of small cultivators had 4.7 live births and those of large cultivators had 5.1 live births.[19] But a study of Kolhapur City fails to show an association of high fertility with higher grade occupations or large income.[20] In nearby Poona District, as one ascends the occupational ladder, fertility declines in the city but remains constant in the non-city area.[21] In the neighboring districts of Nasik and Kolaba the fertility rates of urban and rural women do not differ according to the occupational or income status of their husbands.[22]

A study of couples in 275 villages of the Punjab, who had been married at least ten years, also shows virtually no difference in fertility among occupational and income groups. In not a single village was the correlation coefficient for fertility and income above 0.19.[23] On the other hand, Kingsley Davis, using data from the 1931 Census of India, found variations among occupational groups in their ratios of children 0–6 years of age to women 14–43 years of age. Fertility was higher in the households of agricultural laborers and artisans than in those of traders, professionals, and non-agricultural laborers.

[18] C. Chandrasekharan, *op. cit.*, pp. 8–9.

[19] *Ibid.*

[20] N. V. Sovani, *The Social Survey of Kolhapur City, Part I—Population and Fertility*, Poona: The Gokhale Institute of Politics and Economics, Publication No. 18, 1948, pp. 57–60.

[21] V. M. Dandekar and K. Dandekar, *op. cit.*, pp. 64, 96–97.

[22] N. V. Sovani and K. Dandekar, *op. cit.*, pp. 77–79.

[23] S. P. Jain, *Relationship between Fertility and Economic and Social Status in the Punjab*, Lahore: Punjab Board of Economic Inquiry, Publication No. 64, 1939.

Of all occupational classes, cultivators (owners and tenants) were least fertile. But the differences, which are quite small, almost disappear when widows and spinsters are excluded in computing the ratios.[24] A major deficiency of this study, stemming from the absence of desired cross-tabulations in the census data, was the grouping of castes on the basis of the occupation followed by a *majority* of their members in order to form the above-mentioned occupational classes.

Two studies provide limited information on the fertility patterns among women differentiated according to their own occupational status rather than that of their husbands. The Poona Survey reveals that the fertility rate of women doing housework, as compared with that of women employed outside the home, is high in the city but low in the non-city area.[25] But in Nasik and Kolaba Districts, fertility is independent of the woman's employment status.[26]

The relation of land ownership to fertility is treated in the report of the National Sample Survey, Government of India. Among women married at least twelve years, the wives of the largest landowners have the highest fertility. But the differences between the groups are small, and the relationship of land ownership to fertility is not linear.[27]

## EDUCATIONAL STATUS

The studies which have analyzed the relationship between fertility and educational status differ in their findings. Literate and illiterate women in urban and rural Poona District are found to be little differentiated in reproductive performance.[28] From census data, Kingsley Davis finds that there is a curvilinear relationship between the number of living children in various castes and the percentage of their women who are literate.[29] The Survey of Mysore reports the following differences in average completed family size among women whose

[24] K. Davis, *The Population of India and Pakistan*, Princeton: Princeton University Press, 1951, pp. 74–75.
[25] V. M. Dandekar and K. Dandekar, *op. cit.*, pp. 65, 102.
[26] N. V. Sovani and K. Dandekar, *op. cit.*, p. 79.
[27] A. D. Gupta (*et al*) *op. cit.*, p. 14.
[28] V. M. Dandekar and K. Dandekar, *op. cit.*, pp. 65, 103.
[29] K. Davis, *op. cit.*, p. 75.

first marriage was unbroken: six children for those having less than a high school education; five children for those having a high school education; and two children for those having a college education. But the latter two groups are so small that their influence on the general fertility rate is hardly perceptible.[30]

It is evident from our review that the several studies do not show a consistent relationship between fertility performance and differentiations among persons in either residence, religious and caste affiliation, economic status, or educational achievement. Some of the inconsistency may be attributed to the differences among investigators in measuring fertility and defining dimensions of social status. For example, Kingsley Davis and the United Nations-Government of India team differ radically in their methods of relating fertility to educational achievement. As previously mentioned, the former relates the number of living children in various castes to the percentage of women who are literate. The latter relates completed family size to three levels of educational achievement: below high school, high school, and college. Differences in method are not, however, the sole explanation of the inconsistency. The Gokhale Institute had employed approximately the same methods to analyze fertility patterns in four districts of Western India, but has not found a consistent relationship between fertility and variations in social status. Some of the inconsistency, therefore, indicates that the patterns of differential fertility may vary slightly from one locality to another.

## BASIS OF DIFFERENTIAL FERTILITY

Implicit in discussions of fertility patterns is the expectation that differences in fertility will exist among social strata. At this point brief attention may be given to the reasons for this expectation.

This expectation is based upon the observation of differences among social strata in physical factors and cultural practices, or a combination of the two, which are assumed to affect the frequency of their exposure to the risks of pregnancy. Among the physical or biological factors are: sterility in either the male or female; serious

[30] A. J. Coale and E. M. Hoover, *op. cit.*, p. 48.

11

illnesses or disabilities which incapacitate individuals for prolonged periods; the age at which menstruation begins; the age at which widowhood usually occurs; and physical separation necessitated by the male's employment. As we indicated earlier, Kingsley Davis observes that fertility variations among social strata are primarily the result of differences among them in the number of widowed and spinster women. Chandrasekharan notes a rise in fertility in those areas where malaria, a disabling illness, has been brought under control.[31] By a report of a rural area near Delhi, about half of the village women do not resume menstruation until a year or more after the termination of a pregnancy.[32]

The cultural factors which presumably affect the frequency of a group's exposure to the risks of pregnancy include: the practice of the woman returning to the parental home for child delivery and prolonged postnatal care; the belief that frequent sexual intercourse is injurious to health; and sexual abstinence during lactation, on specific days of the week, and during long periods of religious observance.[33] According to one writer, "sexual abstinence is expected on all festival occasions (and there are many), on Tuesdays for some castes, on Mondays for others, on Fridays for still others, during whole lunar months at a time, on full-moon days, new-moon days, during menstruation and for some days after, on the day the husband has a shave and a haircut, and the day he has his ritual bath. The extreme is found in orthodox Tanjore, where Brahmins approach their wives on Fridays only."[34] Another cultural factor is the knowledge which a group has of the physiology of reproduction, means of preventing conception, and techniques of interrupting a pregnancy. In addition, differences in fertility among social strata may stem from differences among them in the ages at which couples customarily

[31] C. Chandrasekharan, *op. cit.*, p. 9.

[32] World Health Organization, *Final Report on Pilot Studies in Family Planning*, New Delhi, 1954.

[33] In a study of a village in North India, a researcher observed forty calendrical rites, twenty-five of which revolve primarily around family needs and purposes and require sexual abstinence. See: M. E. Opler, "Family, Anxiety, and Religion in a Community of North India," *Culture and Mental Health*, edited by M. E. Opler, New York: Macmillan, 1959, pp. 273–289.

[34] T. Zinkin, *India Changes*, New York: Oxford University Press, 1958, p. 63.

12

marry, and the kind of family structure to which they belong after marriage. The ways in which these last two factors, age at marriage and family structure, are supposed to affect fertility are discussed in detail in Chapters Three and Four.

## OBJECTIVES OF THIS STUDY

This study of differential fertility is based on a survey of households conducted by the author during January–May 1958 in Nagpur District, which is now politically a part of Bombay State although geographically situated in Central India. Trained interviewers, using a schedule, contacted about one per cent of the households in the rural and urban sections of this district. They obtained information on the marital history, fertility performance, and socio-economic characteristics of the couple or, in unusual cases, the person who was defined by the occupants as the head of the household.

The objectives of this study are of several kinds. The main one is to determine whether the number of children ever born (fertility) varies among women who are differentiated: by place of residence, religious or caste affiliation, employment status, and educational achievement; and by the type of occupation, annual earnings, land ownership, and educational achievement of their husbands. Our second objective is to learn whether the differences or similarities among subgroups in fertility are related to their age distributions. In order to accomplish this objective, it will be necessary to express the fertility performance of each subgroup by a statistical measure which is not influenced by the subgroup's age composition. The measure employed in this study is the "weighted mean." The procedures used in its computation are described in detail in Chapter Five.

The weighted means for the various subgroups are also used in connection with the other three major objectives of this study. As we mentioned earlier, variations among social strata in fertility may stem from differences among them in age at marriage, family structure, or the use of techniques to prevent conception or to interrupt pregnancy. Our third objective, therefore, is to determine whether

13

there is any connection between the fertility averages of subgroups in each social category and the ages at which their women usually marry. In order to perform this analysis, it will be necessary as a preliminary step to compute the median age at marriage for women in each subgroup. It will also be of interest to ascertain whether age at marriage has changed over time. Our fourth objective is to determine whether the fertility averages of subgroups are related to the percentage of their women who have membership in a joint family.

The fifth and last major objective is related to birth control techniques. Consideration is given to the relation between the fertility averages of subgroups and the percentage of their couples using birth control devices. We are also interested in learning the degree to which the several social strata have knowledge of birth control techniques and are interested in family limitation, and the reasons why they are interested in family limitation.

The sources of data for this study and the methods by which the data were collected are given detailed consideration in the next chapter.

14

# Methodology

THIS study of differential fertility employs essentially the same methodological procedures as those used in the majority of demographic investigations in India. These include the use of an interview schedule, interviewing techniques, and a sampling procedure. In addition, some method is ordinarily devised whereby valid comparisons of the fertility performances of social strata can be made. Our method of handling this problem was described in Chapter One. In this chapter, consideration is given first to the interview schedule and interviewing technique and then to the sampling procedure and the adequacy of the sample.

## THE INTERVIEW

### THE INTERVIEW SCHEDULE

A schedule[1] containing 92 major questions was devised by the author as a method of ensuring that interviewers would obtain complete and uniform data. After each question, there was a blank space for recording the interviewee's response. The questions were "open-ended" rather than "structured" and, consequently, the categories presented later are the result of our classification of individual responses.

The arrangement of questions on the schedule was based on several considerations. First, it was felt that the cooperation of the interviewee could be obtained rather easily if we began with less personal and controversial questions and gradually moved to questions of an intimate nature. Questions dealing with religion, caste, and other socio-economic characteristics constitute the former kind whereas

[1] The schedule which we used is not reproduced in this study because of its length. We wish to inform our readers who are interested in its structure that it is virtually identical to the schedule employed by V. M. Dandekar and K. Dandekar and reproduced in their study, *Survey of Fertility and Mortality in Poona District*, 1953.

15

those dealing with birth control practices constitute the latter kind. Secondly, a number of duplicate questions were included on the schedule and these had to be placed at a distance from one another in order to ensure that the respondent's answer to one did not influence his answer to the other. These duplicates or "cross-checks" are employed to measure the reliability (consistency) of the interviewee's response. They are especially important in surveys which seek numerical data from populations having a low percentage of literate persons. Checks are made on responses to questions pertaining to age, age at marriage, husband-wife difference in age at marriage, and the number of children ever born.

## THE INTERVIEW PROCESS

The interviewers employed in this study were male and female undergraduate and graduate students of social science at Nagpur University, and students at the Government Medical College, Nagpur City. All of them were skilled in English, the language used on the schedule, and the majority spoke Marathi or Hindi as well, the major languages of Central India. In addition, some of the interviewers knew Tamil, Telegu or other languages which were spoken by a few interviewees. Altogether 35 interviewers participated in the survey for varying lengths of time.

Initially, the interviewers were informed of the purposes of the survey, and acquainted with the meaning of each item on the schedule and the rationale behind the arrangement of the items. They were given brief instructions, if necessary, in ways of establishing rapport with interviewees and in interviewing techniques. Each interviewer was then asked to conduct a few trial interviews, and if these were found satisfactory he was invited to continue on the survey team. Periodic reviews were held with the entire team in order to ensure continued and clear understanding of the items on the schedule, and to obtain suggestions regarding useful probe questions and methods of obtaining complete cooperation from various kinds of interviewees.

As we mentioned previously, interviews were conducted with the head of the household and his spouse at their place of residence. The interviewees were informed of the purpose of the survey, told that

16

they were part of a large group of persons who were being contacted, and were assured that the information given by them would be treated confidentially. It was, of course, our intent to conduct interviews in privacy but this was nearly impossible in most households because of limited space and/or the presence of other members of the household or community. However, the lack of privacy proved not to be an obstruction. Most interviewees did not place a high value on privacy and were quite willing to provide, in an apparently candid manner, information about themselves even though neighbors were present.

In general, the interviewees in both the city and non-city areas were most cooperative. Only a few of them refused outright to provide any of the desired information. A small number of other persons agreed to the interview, answered the initial questions, and then broke off the interview when subsequent questions, especially those pertaining to birth control, proved too difficult or personal for them to answer. In addition, a few persons who were most cooperative in attitude requested assistance in answering questions requiring a numerical response. Three techniques were used to assist them. First, each interviewer had a calendar of the important events which had occurred in this area of India between 1875 and 1940. Through questioning whether the interviewee was a child, youth or adult, or married or single person at the time of particular events, the interviewer might reasonably estimate the interviewee's current age or age at marriage. Secondly, the interviewee might be assisted by other persons in the household or community who were well acquainted with his life history. It was found that these informants could often clearly indicate such matters as the total births, age, and earnings of the interviewee. Lastly, the interviewee might be asked to estimate his age or other characteristics by comparing himself with a literate person whom he knew and whom we knew or could interview. Except, then, for the few persons who required assistance and the few who were uncooperative, our interviewees willingly provided complete and reliable information.

Reliability or consistency of response was measured by two procedures. First, as we mentioned earlier, the schedule contained a number of duplicate or "cross-check" questions. For example, if an interviewee stated that he and his spouse had had a total of eight births, then we would check this against his answers to questions concerning the number of male births and the number of female births. A second procedure was to have our field supervisors or best interviewers repeat some of the interviews of our less able interviewers. Examination of these procedures shows that highly reliable data were obtained from most interviewees. But, reliability does not mean that accurate information was obtained; it only means that a given interviewee was consistent in his responses. The only check on the accuracy or truthfulness of an answer to a particular question was the interviewer's judgment of whether the answer was reasonable in view of the interviewee's general situation or some other criterion.

## THE SAMPLING TECHNIQUE

The persons who provided data for this study represent about one per cent of the heads of households in Nagpur District.

### THE SAMPLING AREA

Nagpur District is nearly the geographic center of India and is situated at the crossing of north-south (Delhi-Madras) and east-west (Calcutta-Bombay) highways, railways, and airways. By the 1951 census, it has a population of 1,234,556 persons and an area of 3834 square miles. About 47 per cent of this population is concentrated in Nagpur City and the twelve towns of this district, which together occupy an area of only 46 square miles.

The City dominates not only the district but also a much wider area. It has no equal for 200 miles in any direction. Until the reorganization of states in 1955, Nagpur City was the capital of Madhya Pradesh State. In 1958, the time of the survey, many of the state offices were still located here. It is a major educational center, containing Nagpur University, which has an enrollment of roughly 9000, two large technological institutes, and the Government Medical College and Hospital, which is reputedly the largest medical center in Asia. There are eleven private hospitals, 43 municipal dispensaries, six municipal maternity homes, and several child welfare centers and nursing homes. In addition to governmental, educational, and medical activities, the City is engaged in industry and commerce. Handloom weaving, textile mills, and the marketing of oranges, other citrus fruits and cotton, provide considerable employment.

In addition to this city of about a half-million population, there are twelve towns and 1667 villages in the district. Their inhabitants are ordinarily engaged in agriculture, fruit growing, handloom weaving, and mining.

A study of fertility patterns in this area of India is important not only because it provides an opportunity to sample a large city, and several towns and villages, but also for several other reasons. First and foremost, a variety of studies of fertility differentials in various parts of India is urgently needed to overcome gaps in our general knowledge.[2] Secondly, this area is especially important because it is situated in what is known as "old India." It is an area of long settlement and one which has not been influenced to any great extent by major centers such as Delhi or Bombay or by contact with Western nations. Although Nagpur City resembles new cities of comparable size in some of its economic features, it differs radically in other respects. "The city has developed as extensions of villages, continuous for long distances without wide roads, and with hardly any open spaces."[3] It has few markets worth mentioning and the weekly markets, to which villagers bring their produce, still operate. The milk supply, except for the Telekhedi Co-operative Dairy, is supplied by urban and rural gaolis (cowherds). There is a municipal and an inter-municipal bus system but most of the transport is by foot, cycle, or rickshaw. Throughout the entire district, forms of dress, eating, manners, and thought are traditional or conservative. Most of the population of India resides in similar areas or those of "old India" and it is they rather than the inhabitants of new centers who will largely determine the future course of fertility in India.

[2] C. Chandrasekharan, "India's Population Problem," pp. 1–2.
[3] Nagpur Improvement Trust, *Master Plan of Nagpur 1953*, Nagpur: Government Printing, Madhya Pradesh, 1954, p. 12.

19

## SAMPLE SIZE AND SELECTION

It was evident from the beginning of the study that limitations of time, money, and staff would permit us, under the most favorable circumstances, to contact about one per cent of the households in the city, towns, and villages of Nagpur District. We felt, however, that if a sample of this size were selected in an adequate manner, we would obtain a clear picture of the fertility differentials present in this area of India. The selection of households in the city was thus guided by two considerations: (1) the need to contact persons from all wards in order that the sample not reflect peculiar ecological patterns; and (2) the need, in view of our limited resources, to concentrate the interviewing. These objectives were achieved by several steps. First, the city was stratified by wards and the number of occupied houses[4] for each ward was recorded. In order to obtain information from at least one per cent of the households in each ward, we decided to select two per cent of them for inclusion in the original sample. The size of the original sample was based on the assumptions that some couples would not cooperate and that other couples would not be located.

Next we worked out a procedure whereby the households selected would come from different parts of a ward and yet would permit our interviewers to concentrate their efforts. This involved selecting households in clusters of five (or six), each cluster coming from a different part of the ward. The procedure used in each of the 42 wards may be most clearly indicated by using Ward 2, Sangam, as an illustration. Sangam had a total of 1602 occupied houses, and, therefore 32 (two per cent) of them were to be included in the original sample. Since the 32 households were to be selected in clusters of five (or six), this meant that six clusters were needed. By dividing the total number of households (1602) by the number of clusters (six), we arrived at a figure, 267, which could be used to evenly subdivide Sangam into six groups of households. The range in household

---

[4] In this study, "occupied house" and "household" are treated as equivalent terms, whereas, in fact, they are not. An occupied house may contain one or more households. However, by our inspection of the National Register of Citizens, we have gained the impression that the total number of households does not greatly exceed the total number of occupied houses in Nagpur District.

numbers for each group in Sangam was, therefore, as follows: 1–267; 268–534; 535–801; 802–1068; 1069–1335; and 1336–1602. In selecting one cluster from each of these groups, we randomly picked the number of the first household and then listed the next four consecutive numbers.

After recording the household numbers selected from each ward, we then turned to the National Register of Citizens. This report of the Census Commission lists by serial number the name and address of each household that was contacted by a census worker in 1951. We therefore listed on our sheets the names and addresses of the households whose serial numbers corresponded with the numbers which we had selected. The exact location of each address was fixed by consulting the ward maps attached to the register or those of the Nagpur Improvement Trust. Three wards had to be omitted from our sample because the register and/or map for them were missing.

Our interviewers were provided with the addresses of the selected households and were instructed to interview until they had covered half of them (one per cent of the total households in each ward). They were also told the head couple residing at each address was to be interviewed and that this couple should be interviewed even if it was not the one which resided at the address at the time of the 1951 census. Furthermore, if the 1951 residents had moved to a new address, the interviewer was not to make any effort to locate them because our sample was based upon household addresses rather than household names. Our objective of interviewing one per cent of the households in each ward was usually achieved or surpassed despite the fact that a few couples were uncooperative and certain dwellings could not be located. The inability to locate some dwellings stemmed from two circumstances: (1) some addresses listed in the register were those of temporary dwellings (huts) and by the time of our survey, these places had been demolished or relocated; and (2) the house numbers in the register were those assigned temporarily by the census commission and they were no longer affixed to some dwellings. The number and percentage of households which we contacted and interviewed in each ward are presented in Table 3.

21

# TABLE 3
## Number and Percentage of Total Households Interviewed in Each Ward of Nagpur City

| WARD No. | Name | Total Households* | HOUSEHOLDS INTERVIEWED Number | Percentage | WARD No. | Name | Total Households* | HOUSEHOLDS INTERVIEWED Number | Percentage |
|---|---|---|---|---|---|---|---|---|---|
| 1 | Dhantoli | 2070 | 34 | 1.6 | 22 | Bagad Ganja | 3110 | 24 | 0.8 |
| 2 | Sangam | 1602 | 19 | 1.2 | 23 | Lalgangi | 2437 | 34 | 1.4 |
| 3 | Somwar Bazar | 1558 | — | — | 24 | Mehadi Bagh | 2436 | — | — |
| 4 | Sitabuldi | 1566 | 18 | 1.2 | 25 | Reshim Bazar | 1903 | 26 | 1.4 |
| 5 | Factory Ward | 2056 | 25 | 1.2 | 26 | Jaganath Mandir | 1620 | — | — |
| 6 | Model Mills | 3188 | 37 | 1.2 | 27 | Panch Pawali | 1340 | 26 | 1.9 |
| 7 | Jat Tarodi | 2320 | 27 | 1.2 | 28 | Mominpura | 1193 | 16 | 1.3 |
| 8 | Siraspeth | 3610 | 44 | 1.2 | 29 | Mayo Hospital | 1570 | 21 | 1.3 |
| 9 | Mahal | 2899 | 45 | 1.6 | 30 | Boriyapur | 1180 | 14 | 1.2 |
| 10 | Sakkardara | 2284 | 26 | 1.1 | 31 | Bhankheda | 1446 | 19 | 1.3 |
| 11 | Mangalwari | 2544 | 28 | 1.1 | 32 | Lashhari Bagh | 1650 | 33 | 2.0 |
| 12 | Budhawar Bazar | 1702 | 22 | 1.3 | 33 | Motibagh | 3749 | 38 | 1.0 |
| 13 | Kotwali | 2180 | 25 | 1.2 | 34 | Chawani Nayabasti | 2162 | 42 | 1.9 |
| 14 | Shukrawar Tank | 784 | 15 | 1.9 | 35 | Indora | 2634 | 42 | 1.6 |
| 15 | Santra Market | 2407 | 48 | 2.0 | 36 | Gaddi Godam | 1548 | 20 | 1.3 |
| 16 | Khadan | 1674 | 20 | 1.2 | 37 | Mohan Nayar | 1625 | 17 | 1.1 |
| 17 | Ganjakhet | 1059 | 11 | 1.0 | 38 | Sadar South | 759 | 12 | 1.6 |
| 18 | Namak Ganja | 1326 | 20 | 1.5 | 39 | Sadar North | 1513 | 25 | 1.7 |
| 19 | Ayachit Mandir | 2098 | 24 | 1.1 | 40 | Civil Lines | 1589 | 17 | 1.1 |
| 20 | Balaji Mandir | 2326 | 22 | 1.0 | 41 | Dharampeth | 3645 | 58 | 1.6 |
| 21 | Itwara | 2542 | 32 | 1.3 | 42 | Lendhara | 1794 | 17 | 1.0 |

* Census of India 1951, Madhya Pradesh, *Nagpur District Census Handbook*, by J. D. Kerawalla, Nagpur: Government Printing, Madhya Pradesh, 1952, p. 174.

Our procedure for selecting sample households in the towns and villages was a very simple one. Altogether Nagpur District has twelve towns and 1667 villages and it was, of course, impossible with our resources to select households from each one of them. We therefore decided to select one per cent of the households in each type of residence (town or village) but to obtain all of our cases from a few towns and villages. Households in Kalmeshwar and Mopha were selected to represent town dwellers. Our procedure in this case was to place our interviewers in different sections of Kalmeshwar and Mopha, inform them of the number of interviews which were to be completed, and ask them to contact people who varied in social circumstances. Our two field supervisors were, of course, always present to ensure that the latter instruction was followed.[5] Interviews were completed with 198 of the 1305 households in Kalmeshwar and 165 of the 1230 households in Mopha. The 363 (198 plus 165) households constitute over one per cent of all households present in towns of Nagpur District.

Interviews were conducted with the head couple or person in the households of 23 villages. The main considerations in choosing the particular villages were that they should come from different tahsils (administrative units), and should vary in (a) size, (b) distance from the city, and (c) accessibility to main roads. A map of the district was employed to select villages which fitted these conditions. Our procedure was to contact every household in the small villages whereas in the few very large villages, we followed the procedure used in the two towns. Table 4 presents the villages by name, tahsil, number of households, and the number of households interviewed.

Altogether 2719 of the total households in the district were contacted and interviewed. The information given on their schedules was found useful for our purpose, a study of differential fertility, in all but 130 instances. Of the 130 schedules which were discarded, 56

---

[5] In the absence of especially close supervision, the interviewers might have selected persons who for various reasons were congenial to them, i.e. persons who were neat in appearance or pleasant in manner, and persons who were of medium or high social status. The supervisors are of the opinion that they were able to prevent this type of bias from entering into the selection of respondents by the interviewers.

were eliminated because they contained either very incomplete or obviously inaccurate information. The other 74 schedules were not used because the head of the household was a separated person in

TABLE 4

Number of Households Interviewed in Selected Villages of Nagpur District

| Tahsil | Village | Total Households* | Number of Households Interviewed |
|--------|---------|-------------------|----------------------------------|
| Saoner | Patansaongi | 802 | 170 |
|  | Waghoda | 75 | 31 |
|  | New Gujarkhedi | Not listed | 30 |
| Nagpur | Ambazari | 6 | 15 |
|  | Mahadulla | 63 | 73 |
|  | Somalwada | 285 | 36 |
|  | Babulkheda | 62 | 40 |
|  | Gumgaon | 744 | 100 |
|  | Borgaon | 282 | 62 |
|  | Pardi | 67 | 43 |
| Ramtek | Mouda | 512 | 140 |
|  | Khaperkheda | 25 | 28 |
|  | Chicha Bhuwan | 44 | 49 |
|  | Wanjra | 47 | 41 |
| Umrer | Panchgaon | 247 | 119 |
|  | Champa | 86 | 34 |
|  | Kalmna | 53 | 39 |
|  | Dahegaon | 57 | 65 |
|  | Sonegaon | 40 | 26 |
| Katol | Parsodi | 52 | 46 |
|  | Dongargaon | 27 | 19 |
|  | Mohadi | 62 | 58 |
|  | Umari | 50 | 37 |

* Census of India, 1951, Madhya Pradesh, *Nagpur District Census Handbook*, by J. D. Kerawalla, Nagpur: Government Printing, Madhya Pradesh, 1952, pp. 174–220.

sixteen instances and a single person in 58 instances. Of the single (never married), four were female and 54 were male. All of the females resided in Nagpur City, and three of them, who were between 20 and 24 years of age, were in nursing training at the Government

Medical College. The fourth female was 28 years of age and employed by the post and telegraph department. Of the 54 males, 34 resided in the city, ten resided in a town, and ten resided in a village. Except for their concentration in the city and in the 20–29 age group, the characteristics (religion, caste, etc.) of the single males are distributed in roughly the same manner as those of married males.

The elimination of 130 schedules leaves us with a final sample of 2589 households, or about one per cent of the total in the district.

TABLE 5

Distribution of Households by Marital Status and Sex of Head Person

| MARITAL STATUS AND SEX OF HEAD PERSON | NUMBER OF HOUSEHOLDS | TOTAL LIVING | |
|---|---|---|---|
| | | Husbands | Wives |
| Female | | | |
|   Widowed | 96 | — | 96 |
| Male | | | |
|   Widowed | 159 | 159 | — |
|   Married | | | |
|     One wife | 2297 | 2297 | 2297 |
|     Two wives | 36 | 36 | 72 |
|     Four wives | 1 | 1 | 4 |
| Total | 2589 | 2493 | 2469 |

This sample provides us with rather complete and accurate information on the characteristics of 2493 males and 2469 females who were defined as the head or the wife of the head of a household. The difference between the number of males and females results from the manner in which the heads of households are distributed by marital status. As Table 5 shows, the head of household was a widow in 96 instances and a widower in 159 instances. In the remaining 2334 households, the head person was a male who had one or more living spouses.

## ADEQUACY OF THE SAMPLE

A sample of one per cent which has been selected in a random or stratified, random manner usually provides an accurate picture of how social characteristics and fertility patterns are distributed in the total population. When a sample, such as ours, is not random, then it is important to assess its adequacy. This assessment can ordinarily be made by comparing the distribution of characteristics (religion, caste, etc.) in the sample and in the relevant census report. However, for several reasons, comparisons of this order cannot, in our case, be completely valid. First, our sample refers to the head of household or his spouse, units which are generally missing in census materials.

TABLE 6

Residence of Survey Households and Total Households, Nagpur District

| PLACE OF RESIDENCE | NUMBER OF HOUSEHOLDS | | PERCENTAGE OF HOUSEHOLDS | |
| | Survey | District* | Survey | District |
| --- | --- | --- | --- | --- |
| City | 983 | 84,698 | 38.1 | 34.3 |
| Town | 344 | 24,954 | 13.3 | 10.1 |
| Village | 1262 | 137,126 | 48.6 | 55.6 |
| Total | 2589 | 246,778 | 100.0 | 100.0 |

* SOURCE: Census of India 1951, Madhya Pradesh, *Nagpur District Census Handbook*, by J. D. Kerawalla, Nagpur: Government Printing, Madhya Pradesh, 1952, p. 2.

Secondly, we have presented the characteristics of married adults whereas the census in presenting the same characteristics often fails to distinguish between adults and non-adults, and between married and unmarried persons. Lastly, the classificatory schemes used in this study are not always identical to those found in the census report for Nagpur District. We have tried to overcome the differences between our study and the census report by rearranging, insofar as it was possible, the data of one or the other. Still, as subsequent tables show, all of the comparisons which we make are not completely valid.

The several comparisons show that our sample is, in some respects, a very adequate representation of the general population. In other respects, it is rather inadequate. With respect to residence, the sample contains a larger percentage of both city and town households than are found in the general population. The difference is not, however, excessive, and is the result of our contact with more than one per cent of the city and town households and with slightly less than one per cent of those in the villages.

The distributions of religions and castes in the sample are almost identical to their distributions in the general population. According to Table 7, the percentage of Hindus and Buddhists is 93.4 for the sample and 92.8 for the general population. Muslims, Jains, Sikhs,

TABLE 7

Religion of Survey Households and of Total Population, Nagpur District

| | NUMBER | | PERCENTAGE | |
| RELIGION | Survey | District* | Survey | District |
| --- | --- | --- | --- | --- |
| Hindu | 2,147 | 1,144,411 | 82.9⎫ | 92.8 |
| Buddhist | 271 | 149 | 10.5⎭ | |
| Muslim | 109 | 70,789 | 4.2 | 5.7 |
| Jain | 19 | 5,216 | 0.7 | 0.4 |
| Sikh | 7 | 2,394 | 0.3 | 0.2 |
| Parsee | 4 | 1,706 | 0.2 | 0.1 |
| Christian | 32 | 9,803 | 1.2 | 0.8 |
| Other | — | 88 | — | 0.0 |
| Total | 2,589 | 1,234,556 | 100.0 | 100.0 |

* SOURCE: Census of India 1951, Madhya Pradesh, *Nagpur District Census Handbook*, by J. D. Kerawalla, Nagpur: Government Printing, Madhya Pradesh, 1952, Table D II—Religion, p. 149.

TABLE 8

Survey Households and Total Population, Nagpur District, Belonging to Scheduled Castes

| | NUMBER | | PERCENTAGE | |
| | Survey | District** | Survey | District |
| --- | --- | --- | --- | --- |
| Scheduled Castes | 493* | 223,695 | 19.0* | 18.1 |
| Total | 2589 | 1,234,556 | 100.0 | 100.0 |

* Included are the Buddhists who were Mahars, a scheduled caste, before their conversion after 1951.

** SOURCE: Census of India 1951, Madhya Pradesh, *Nagpur District Census Handbook*, by J. D. Kerawalla, Nagpur: Government Printing, Madhya Pradesh, 1952, Table D II—Scheduled Castes, Scheduled Tribes and Anglo-Indians, p. 150.

TABLE 9
Occupations of Male Heads of Households, Survey, and of Total
Self-Supporting Males, Nagpur District

| OCCUPATIONAL GROUP | NUMBER OF MALES Survey | District* | PERCENTAGE OF MALES Survey | District |
|---|---|---|---|---|
| Agricultural | 656 | 80,887 | 26.3 | 25.6 |
| Other | 1837 | 235,164 | 73.7 | 74.4 |
| Total | 2493 | 316,051 | 100.0 | 100.0 |

* SOURCE: Census of India 1951, Madhya Pradesh, *Nagpur District Census Handbook*, by J. D. Kerawalla, Nagpur: Government Printing, Madhya Pradesh, 1952, Economic Table B I—Livelihood Classes and Sub-classes, pp. 8–13.

Parsees, and Christians are also about equally represented in the two groups. Insofar as caste affiliation is concerned, 19.0 per cent of the sample and 18.1 per cent of all persons belong to the Scheduled Castes. Unfortunately, the census report does not permit a more detailed comparison of caste groupings.

The sample and general population may also be compared with respect to three measures of economic status: occupation of the male, employment of the female, and land ownership of the male. According to Table 9, the ratio of agricultural to non-agricultural occupations is about 1:3 in each group. The percentage of females having employment (i.e. earning wages) is, however, higher in the

TABLE 10
Employment Status of Wives of Heads of Households, Survey, and
of Total Adult Females, Nagpur District

| EMPLOYMENT STATUS | NUMBER OF FEMALES Survey | District* | PERCENTAGE OF FEMALES Survey | District |
|---|---|---|---|---|
| Unemployed | 2141 | 248,135 | 86.7 | 92.8 |
| Employed | 328 | 19,290 | 13.3 | 7.2 |
| Total | 2469 | 267,425 | 100.0 | 100.0 |

* SOURCE: Census of India, 1951, Madhya Pradesh, *Nagpur District Census Handbook*, by J. D. Kerawalla, Nagpur: Government Printing, Madhya Pradesh, 1952, Economic Table 5 III—Employers, Employees and Independent Workers, and Table C I—Household Size and Composition, pp. 55 and 105.

sample than in the general population, the figures being 13.3 and 7.2 respectively. In the case of land ownership, approximately 58.0 per cent of each group is landless. But, large land owners, those having ten or more acres, constitute 25.4 per cent of the sample males and only 15.8 per cent of all males.

TABLE 11

Land Ownership of Male Heads of Households, Survey, and of Total Self-Supporting Males, Nagpur District

| LAND OWNERSHIP (IN ACRES) | NUMBER OF MALES | | PERCENTAGE OF MALES | |
|---|---|---|---|---|
| | Survey | District* | Survey | District |
| None | 1,439 | 184,323 | 57.5 | 58.3 |
| 1–2 | 88 | 29,506 | 3.6 | 9.3 |
| 3–4 | 126 | 18,124 | 5.1 | 5.7 |
| 5–9 | 207 | 34,345 | 8.4 | 10.9 |
| 10–19 | 312 | 29.854 | 12.6 | 9.5 |
| 20–49 | 217 | 16,449 | 8.8 | 5.2 |
| 50–99 | 71 | 2,657 | 2.9 | 0.8 |
| 100–199 | 21 | 676 | 0.9 | 0.2 |
| 200 or more | 12 | 117 | 0.2 | 0.1 |
| Total | 2,493 | 316,051 | 100.0 | 100.0 |

* SOURCE: Census of India, 1951, Madhya Pradesh, *Nagpur District Census Handbook*, by J. D. Kerawalla, Nagpur: Government Printing, Madhya Pradesh, 1952, p. 236.

Males in the two groups differ considerably in their educational achievement. In the sample, 39.6 per cent are illiterate, 31.7 per cent have primary schooling, and 28.7 per cent have more than primary schooling. The respective figures for the general population are 60.3, 31.9, and 7.8. The females in the two groups are, however, quite similar in educational achievement. The percentage of illiterates and primary educates, respectively, are 77.6 and 13.6 for the sample, and 85.0 and 12.3 for the general population.

Insofar as age is concerned, our male heads of households are older than married males in the general population, the medians being 40.8 years and 36.9 years. The difference is not excessive and is primarily due to the high percentage (17.6) of total males and the low percentage (5.3) of sample males in the age group, 15–24 years.

TABLE 12

Educational Level of Male Heads of Households, Survey, and of Total Males Over Four Years of Age, Nagpur District

| EDUCATIONAL LEVEL | NUMBER OF MALES | | PERCENTAGE OF MALES | |
|---|---|---|---|---|
| | Survey | District* | Survey | District |
| None | 986 | 332,518 | 39.6 | 60.3 |
| Primary | 789 | 175,762 | 31.7 | 31.9 |
| Middle | 313 | 18,946 | 12.6 | 3.5 |
| Matriculation or High School | 270 | 13,165 | 10.9 | 2.4 |
| College | 135 | 10,368 | 5.2 | 1.9 |
| Total | 2493 | 550,759 | 100.0 | 100.0 |

* SOURCE: Census of India 1951, Madhya Pradesh, *Nagpur District Census Handbook*, by J. D. Kerawalla, Nagpur: Government Printing, Madhya Pradesh, 1952, Table C IV—Age and Literacy, and Table D VII—Livelihood Classes by Educational Standards, pp. 126 and 161–170.

Females are more nearly similar, the median ages being 32.0 years for the sample and 30.8 years for all married females. As in the case of males, the difference between them is mainly attributable to their representations in the 15–24 year group. Whereas 32.5 per cent of all females fall into this category, only 20.7 per cent of the sample females do so.

TABLE 13

Educational Level of Wives of Heads of Households, Survey, and of Total Females Over Four Years of Age, Nagpur District

| EDUCATIONAL LEVEL | NUMBER OF FEMALES | | PERCENTAGE OF FEMALES | |
|---|---|---|---|---|
| | Survey | District* | Survey | District |
| None | 1,914 | 444,025 | 77.6 | 85.0 |
| Primary | 331 | 64,361 | 13.4 | 12.3 |
| Middle | 108 | 8,817 | 4.4 | 1.7 |
| Matriculation or High School | 86 | 3,003 | 3.4 | 0.6 |
| College | 30 | 2,031 | 1.2 | 0.4 |
| Total | 2,469 | 522,237 | 100.0 | 100.0 |

* SOURCE: Census of India 1951, Madhya Pradesh, *Nagpur District Census Handbook*, by J. D. Kerawalla, Nagpur: Government Printing, Madhya Pradesh, 1952, Table C IV—Age and Literacy and Table D VII—Livelihood Classes by Educational Standards, pp. 126 and 161–170.

## TABLE 14
Age Distribution of Male Heads of Households, Survey, and of the Total Married Males Over Fourteen Years of Age, Nagpur District

| | NUMBER OF MALES | | PERCENTAGE OF MALES | |
| AGE GROUPS | Survey | District* | Survey | District |
| --- | --- | --- | --- | --- |
| 15–24 | 132 | 5,084 | 5.3 | 17.6 |
| 25–34 | 707 | 8,002 | 28.3 | 27.8 |
| 35–44 | 700 | 6,979 | 28.1 | 24.2 |
| 45–54 | 491 | 4,772 | 19.8 | 16.6 |
| 55–64 | 291 | 2,400 | 11.7 | 8.3 |
| 65 and over | 172 | 1,600 | 6.8 | 5.5 |
| Total | 2,493 | 28,837 | 100.0 | 100.0 |

* SOURCE: Census of India 1951, Madhya Pradesh, *Nagpur District Census Handbook*, by J. D. Kerawalla, Nagpur: Government Printing, Madhya Pradesh, 1952, Table C III—Age and Civil Condition (which is based on a 10 per cent sample), p. 120.

Lastly, we have compared the females in the sample and in the general population with respect to place of birth. According to Table 16, the percentage born in Nagpur District is 78.0 for the sample and 80.9 for the general population, a difference which is negligible. They also differ very little in the extent to which their women were born in Madhya Pradesh and adjacent states. The

## TABLE 15
Age Distribution of Wives of Heads of Households, Survey, and of Total Married Females Over Fourteen Years of Age, Nagpur District

| | NUMBER OF FEMALES | | PERCENTAGE OF FEMALES | |
| AGE GROUPS | Survey | District* | Survey | District |
| --- | --- | --- | --- | --- |
| 15–24 | 511 | 8,885 | 20.7 | 32.5 |
| 25–34 | 809 | 8,220 | 32.8 | 30.1 |
| 35–44 | 612 | 5,630 | 24.8 | 20.6 |
| 45–54 | 340 | 3,111 | 13.8 | 11.4 |
| 55–64 | 185 | 1,143 | 7.5 | 5.2 |
| 65 and over | 12 | 326 | 0.4 | 0.2 |
| Total | 2,469 | 27,315 | 100.0 | 100.0 |

* SOURCE: Census of India 1951, Madhya Pradesh, *Nagpur District Census Handbook*, by J. D. Kerawalla, Nagpur: Government Printing, Madhya Pradesh, 1952, Table C III—Age and Civil Condition (which is based on a 10 per cent sample), p. 120.

percentage born in distant states is, however, higher for the sample than the general population, the figures being 6.0 and 0.8, respectively.

It seems appropriate to state again that some of our comparisons, for reasons mentioned earlier, are not wholly valid. With this in mind, the results of our analysis may be briefly noted. First, the sample resembles very closely the general population in the distribution of the following characteristics: residence, religion, and caste

TABLE 16

Place of Birth of Wives of Heads of Households, Survey, and of Total Females, Nagpur District

| | NUMBER OF FEMALES | | PERCENTAGE OF FEMALES | |
| PLACE OF BIRTH | Survey | District* | Survey | District |
|---|---|---|---|---|
| Nagpur District | 1930 | 488,047 | 78.0 | 80.9 |
| Madhya Pradesh (State) | } 354 | 87,567 | } 14.4 | 14.5 |
| Adjacent States | | 15,178 | | 2.5 |
| Other States | 148 | 5,074 | 6.0 | 0.8 |
| Outside India | 37 | 7,491 | 1.6 | 1.3 |
| Total | 2469 | 603,357 | 100.0 | 100.0 |

* SOURCE: Census of India 1951, Madhya Pradesh, *Nagpur District Census Handbook*, by J. D. Kerawalla, Nagpur: Government Printing, Madhya Pradesh, 1952, Table D IV—Migrants, pp. 151–157.

of the households; occupation and land ownership of males; and education, age, and place of birth of females. Secondly, the sample contains an excess of employed females and older males, and deviates most from the general population in its high percentage of educated males. In most respects, then, the sample appears to be an adequate representation of the general population.

Thus far, we have not considered the question: Can one reasonably expect the sample to adequately portray the manner in which fertility patterns are distributed among socio-economic strata in the general population? It is necessary to observe that the adequacy of the sample in this regard is more important than its adequacy with respect to the distribution of various social characteristics. This is so because in a study of differential fertility, it is not particularly important whether Brahmins (or any other group) are over-represented,

32

provided that the Brahmins who appear in the sample are typical with regard to fertility. The question which we have raised requires, then, an answer, but it is a question which cannot be answered on the basis of direct evidence. It may, however, be answered in the affirmative on the basis of indirect evidence. We noted above that the sample adequately portrays the manner in which various social characteristics are distributed in the general population and, on this basis, it seems reasonable to assume that the sample also adequately portrays the fertility patterns existing in the general population.

Our next two chapters are concerned with family structure and age at marriage among the various socio-economic groups. Most of the findings pertaining to these topics will be used in Chapter Five to determine whether fertility differences are associated with variations in family structure and age at marriage. For this part of the analysis, only women whose first marriage was unbroken at the time of the survey and their spouses are considered. At the beginning of this chapter we indicated that direct contact was made with 2469 women. After removing the 96 widowed and 59 remarried ones, we are left with 2314 married women.

# Family Structure
# and Socio-Economic Status

Works on India invariably include the joint-family system among the basic features of Hindu social organization. Among non-Hindus, too, the system is thought to have considerable importance.[1] In contrast to the nuclear family (husband, wife, and children), the joint-family, as an ideal type, usually has most of the following features. In structure, it comprises a married man, his father, his grandfather and his collaterals within three generations.[2] The different kinsmen along with their spouses and children occupy the same dwelling, eat and worship together, and enjoy property in common.[3] They cooperate in economic activity and, even if the members are differentiated occupationally, pool their earnings. The joint-family provides nursing care for the sick and afflicted, social security for the unemployed, and support for the aged. "The care and maintenance of . . . dependents is a moral obligation . . . and is backed by the forces of social prestige and opprobrium."[4] The members of this unit, are, in brief, closely knit together. They share the various routines, problems, and joys of social living, have strong feelings of mutual obligation during crises, and regard self-interest as being identical with family welfare. Their respect for the wisdom and justice of the eldest male permits him and his spouse to render decisions which affect each and every member of the unit. As one writer so aptly states:

"The traditional authority of the head over the junior members of

---

[1] K. M. Kapadia, *Marriage and Family in India*, Second Edition, Bombay: Oxford University Press, 1958, pp. 233–243.

[2] *Ibid.*, p. 264.

[3] From the legal point of view, a joint-family exists when the following conditions are observed: common property and income, co-residence, commensality, co-worship, and the performance of certain rights and obligations. See: I. P. Desai, "The Joint Family in India—An Analysis," *Sociological Bulletin*, Vol. V, No. 2 (September 1956), p. 147.

[4] K. M. Kapadia, *op. cit.*, p. 266.

the family was so awe-inspiring that the juniors never thought of expressing their differences, whatever their convictions might be. The subordination and superordination designed to regulate the lives of the different members in the hierarchy of the joint household, recognition of the family as the unit for all social relationships, the place assigned to the family as a juridical unit in family quarrels—all tended to give the family such enormous influence that the individual lost his identity in it. The social environment never provided an opportunity to the individual to feel he had interests apart from those of the family."[5]

The major aim of this chapter is to indicate the extent to which joint-family living occurs in general and among various socio-economic strata in Central India. For our purpose, a joint-family exists whenever a couple and its married son(s) or the married brother(s) or parents of the male member permanently reside together in the same household. Our findings will serve the end, later, of determining whether fertility patterns in various strata are connected with differences among them in joint-family living. Our second aim is to determine the extent to which the joint-family, rather than the nuclear family, is preferred by various strata. Quite obviously, by our definition of the joint family, the only couples who could express a preference and carry it out by action are those having the above-mentioned primary kin. Therefore, in this study, the degree to which a stratum prefers joint-family living is measured by relating the number of couples living in a joint-family to the number of couples who had (married) primary kin.[6] Lastly, we are interested in learning

[5] *Ibid.*, p. 246.

[6] In the studies of Merchant and Kapadia, cited below, preference for joint-family living has a rather different meaning. It exists whenever a couple, irrespective of its actual or potential family structure, *says* that living in a joint-family is more satisfactory than living in a nuclear family. Our definition differs because we feel that the *action* rather than the *statement* of a couple is a more clear indication of its preference. Our feeling is based, in part, upon the following situation. Kapadia states that "about half of those who never lived in a joint-family" said that they preferred the joint-family to the nuclear family. If one assumes that some of these couples have surviving kin with whom they can form a joint-family, then their statement probably has the following meaning: we prefer the joint-family to the nuclear family and we would live in a joint-family if it were not for the fact that this would mean certain disadvantages which we do not currently experience. For example, such couples may be confronted

35

whether the actual prevalence of joint-family living varies among the old and young couples in each stratum. Our findings are presented after a review of various comments and studies pertaining to the prevalence of joint-family living and the relation of the joint-family to fertility performance in areas other than Central India.

## PREVIOUS STUDIES

### PREVALENCE OF THE JOINT-FAMILY

Although the joint-family is usually presented as the major form of family structure in India, there is a lack of statistical evidence of its prevalence in the general population. Despite the general absence of empirical evidence, especially with reference to the past century or

---

with making a choice between (a) residing in the village of their parents and other kin, living in a joint family, and having low economic status and (b) residing in the city and away from their kinsmen, living in a nuclear family, and having comfortable economic status.

It is our belief that a couple may easily *state* a preference for the joint-family or nuclear family without giving much consideration to the implications of their choice. When the same couple has to express its preference by *action*, the choice may be of a different kind and will be made after much deliberation.

Our definition of preference is based upon what couples *do* rather than what they *say* they would like to do. We have measured preference for joint-family living by relating the number of couples having a joint-family to the number of couples who could have a joint-family (i.e. those couples having surviving kin with whom this structure could be formed). It is our view that couples who select one family form or the other do so not merely on the basis of the desirability of living with or separate from kinsmen but rather on the basis of this desirability and whether it takes precedence over or permits the pursuit or retention of other important economic and social values. Recent studies of the family structure in India show that some couples separate from their kinsmen because educational and economic opportunities in the cities are of greater importance to them than being close to their kinsmen. Of course, at the verbal level, couples may indicate the desirability of living close to or distant from kinsmen as if it can be isolated from other values.

This, then, is the reasoning behind our method of defining preference. The definition may appear very rigid but we feel that it is the best definition under the circumstances. It is somewhat analagous to the situation where you measure the preference of subjects for political candidates by (a) noting the person whom they say they would vote for and (b) noting the person whom they do vote for. When there is a discrepancy, one may argue that preference changed in the interval between the expression (statement) and the action. But one may also argue that the statement, in some cases, was the convenient and easy answer whereas the action reflects more thorough deliberation.

two, laymen and intelligentsia are of the opinion that joint-families are fast dying out.[7] This decline is presumedly a consequence of contacts with Western ideals and patterns, increasing migration from the ancestral home to urban or industrial centers for education or employment, and changes in various laws, especially those pertaining to the status of women and property inheritance.[8] The actual effect of these factors on the joint-family during the past century is, however, purely a matter of conjecture. But there are studies which provide limited information on the current status of the joint-family and quite recent changes in it.

The Census Commissioner of India writes in the 1951 Census: "Such a large proportion of small households (33 per cent in villages and 38 per cent in towns) is a *prima facie* indication that families do not continue to be "joint" according to the traditional custom of the country and the habit of breaking away from the joint-family and setting up separate households is quite strong."[9] This view is criticized by I. P. Desai on two grounds: (1) the statistics indicate that the joint-family is still the major type of family structure in India;[10] and (2) the size of the household is not a valid indicator of whether it contains a nuclear or joint-family.[11] Studies of small populations by members of the sociology department, Bombay University, generally conclude that the joint-family is still a vigorous institution. Of 446 college graduates contacted by K. T. Merchant in 1930–1932, 277 or 62.1 per cent were living in a joint-family. However, only 38.5 per cent of the non-graduates contacted had this living arrangement. Of the non-graduates and graduates who were in a joint-family, 43.2 per cent favored this arrangement, 36.5 per cent were opposed to it, and the remainder were indifferent to it.[12] Of 513 secondary school teachers interviewed by K. M. Kapadia, 57.3 per cent lived in and

[7] K. M. Kapadia, *op. cit.*, p. 259.
[8] For a discussion of the presumed role of these and other factors, see the excellent presentation of K. M. Kapadia in his work cited above, pp. 248–281, and that of A. D. Ross in "Symposium: Caste and Joint Family," *Sociological Bulletin*, Vol. IV, No. 2 (September 1955), pp. 85–96.
[9] Census of India 1951, Vol. I, Part I-A, *Report*, p. 50.
[10] "Symposium: Caste and Joint Family," *op. cit.*, p. 116.
[11] I. P. Desai, *op. cit.*, p. 144.
[12] Cited in K. M. Kapadia, *op. cit.*, p. 259.

37

18.1 per cent used to live in a joint-family. This form of living was preferred by 83.3 per cent of those living in a joint-family, 48.3 per cent of those who used to live in a joint-family, and about half of those who never lived in a joint-family. Of the total group, 61.4 per cent favored the joint-family, 18.1 per cent were opposed to it, and 20.5 per cent failed to express an opinion.[13] On the basis of his data and the earlier study of Merchant, Kapadia estimates that the number of educated Hindus living in a joint-family has declined about five per cent over the past twenty years, but the number of those desiring to live jointly has almost doubled.[14]

Another study of Kapadia's analyzed the structure of 246 families in the town of Navsari, South Gujerat, and the structure of 1099 families in fifteen villages which surround Navsari. He found that 56.5 per cent of the town families and 49.7 per cent of the village ones were still "joint" in structure. In the villages, the joint-family was much more prevalent among the higher castes, but in the town there was no marked correspondence between family type and caste.[15] In a study of 410 households in the small town of Mahuwa, Saurashtra, Desai observed that 47 per cent of them had a joint-family. But the nearly equal occurrence of the nuclear family and joint-family does not mean that they are of equal social significance. By Desai's observation, about three-quarters of the individuals in the community are under the influence of the joint-family.[16] One other study provides very meager information on the status of the joint-family in the large urban community. A pilot study of 50 lower caste and lower class employees in Madras City by A. Aiyappan reveals that only nine or 18.0 per cent of them maintained a joint-family.[17]

### RELATION OF JOINT-FAMILY TO FERTILITY

The joint-family is thought to have considerable bearing on the fertility performance of its members. According to one school of

[13] K. M. Kapadia, "Changing Patterns of Hindu Marriage and Family, [Part] III," *Sociological Bulletin*, Vol. IV, No. 2 (September 1955), pp. 161–162.

[14] K. M. Kapadia, *Marriage and Family in India*, p. 260.

[15] K. M. Kapadia, "Rural Family Patterns," *Sociological Bulletin*, Vol. V, No. 2 (September 1956), pp. 113–114, 124.

[16] I. P. Desai, *op. cit.*, p. 154.

[17] "Symposium: Caste and Joint Family," *op. cit.*, p. 121.

thought, it operates to keep fertility below the level that it would reach if a couple lived separately from its kinsmen, i.e. in a nuclear family. By virtue of the number of people living together, couples are permitted little privacy and hence infrequent opportunities for sexual intercourse. In addition, further restrictions may be imposed by the internal organization of the house and the deliberate controls exercised by other members, especially the elders. The only evidence indicating the operation of these factors is a case illustration provided by Taya Zinkin:

"In the South Punjab, a typical household resembles that of Ram Singh, a Delhi student who invited me to visit his father's prosperous home. The inner courtyard, in which most of the family activities go on, is lined with rooms—the kitchen, a number of storerooms, a cattle room, one room for the women, and one for the men, and, in a corner there is a little room, scarcely the size of a big double-bed. Ram Singh explained that this was the nuptial room. The members of the family have to take turns reserving it. To reserve it too often is frowned upon. Ram Singh said that he could ask for it five times a month, at the most, and this only because he is newly married. 'We have no freedom to talk to our wives' he said bitterly.

"The nuptial room is a practice of the better-off. Even in the cities it is often retained by people who live in modern apartments, partly because dormitories reduce the number of rooms required, partly because they do not have the urge to live as couples. The poorer people live in one room which houses everything—the family, the stores and the cattle.[18]"

Even if living quarters are not crowded and each couple has its own bedroom, the presence of other adults in the home may influence the frequency of sexual intercourse and consequently the level of fertility. Such influence is presumably attributable to actual or anticipated intrusions by the eldest female or other members of the joint-family, who may define all areas of the house as public rather than private.

According to the other school of thought, joint-family living tends to increase rather than decrease the level of fertility. Presumably

[18] T. Zinkin, *India Changes*, New York: Oxford University Press, 1958, pp. 63–64.

this stems from several factors. First, a couple may reproduce without giving much consideration to the economic burden of supporting offspring because this burden is not its alone but that of the entire joint-family. The nuclear family, on the other hand, fosters concern over the relation of earnings to dependents.[19] Such concern, it is thought, would reflect itself in attempts at family limitation by contraceptive techniques or by frequent sexual abstinence. Secondly, in the joint-family, the female is encouraged to reproduce and understands that her acceptance by and security among the husband's kin depends greatly upon her success. This encouragement of many children is presumably associated with the values of large family size. It provides prestige in the community and strength in village politics, and is economically beneficial. The size of the family may mean the difference between prosperity and ruin in the agricultural milieu, especially when farm machinery is expensive or absent and hired labor is beyond one's means.[20] If the joint-family is large, it may be economically advantageous, too, to persons engaged in business or other non-agricultural pursuits.[21]

At present, there is little evidence to support either opinion of the effect of the joint-family on fertility. The one empirical study of this topic, a pilot study conducted in West Bengal, provides rather inconclusive results. According to this study, couples living in the one-generational joint-family have very low fertility in both rural and urban areas. On the other hand, those living in the multi-generational joint-family are highly fertile in the rural area but are relatively infertile in the urban area in comparison with couples living in the one-generational joint-family, the nuclear family, or the household complex.[22]

[19] The persistent efforts of a New Delhi school teacher, living in a nuclear family and awaiting the birth of his first child, to establish an equilibrium between his earnings and anticipated expenses, is a central theme of R. Prawer Jhabvala, in *The Householder*, New York: Norton, 1960.

[20] For a vivid portrayal of the thinking of and problems confronting a poor farmer who is faced with the task of harvesting the crop after all his sons have migrated, see: Kamala Markadanaya, *Nectar in the Sieve*, New York: New American Library, 1956.

[21] K. M. Kapadia, *Marriage and Family in India*, pp. 269–270.

[22] S. J. Poti and S. Dutta, "Social Mobility and Differential Fertility," Unpublished Paper presented at the Third All India Sociological Conference, Agra, February 1958.

## OUR FINDINGS

According to our data, the joint-family structure is not widespread in Central India. Of the 2314 women whose first marriage was unbroken at the time of the survey, only 695 or 30.0 per cent of them had membership in this type of structure. Further, most of them

TABLE 17

Distribution of Couples by Type of Family Structure

| FAMILY STRUCTURE | | COUPLES | |
|---|---|---|---|
| Type | Composition (Married primary kinsmen in addition to head male and his spouse) | Number | Percentage |
| Nuclear | None | 1207 | 52.2 |
| Simple | | | |
| Complex | One parent | 412 | 17.8 |
| Joint | | | |
| Simple | Both parents | 116 | 5.0 |
| | Either brother(s) or son(s) | 334 | 14.5 |
| | Either brother(s) or son(s) and one parent | 156 | 6.8 |
| Complex | Brother(s) and son(s) | 17 | 0.7 |
| | Brother(s), son(s) and one parent | 5 | 0.2 |
| | Both parents, and either brother(s) or son(s) | 65 | 2.7 |
| | Both parents, brother(s) and son(s) | 2 | 0.1 |
| Total | | 2314 | 100.0 |

lived in a joint-family which was simple in form, i.e., one consisting of the head couple and one other married pair (either collaterals or lineals of the male head). As Table 17 shows, about 83 per cent (606/695) of the joint-families are of this nature. This table also provides interesting information on the pattern of leadership in the joint-family. It indicates, contrary to the usual assumption, that the eldest couple is not always defined as the head of the unit. In 183 or 26.3 per cent of the joint-families, both parents are present and occupy a subordinate position.

When couples are distinguished on the basis of age, one finds that joint-family living is more frequent among the old couples, those where the wife is over 35 years of age. According to Table 18, 36.0 per cent of the old couples but only 25.2 per cent of the young ones are living "jointly." On the surface, the difference appears negligible because, as Table 19 shows, a larger percentage of the old couples had

TABLE 18
Number and Percentage of Couples Having Joint Family, by Age of Wife

| FAMILY STRUCTURE | NUMBER | | | PERCENTAGE | | |
| | Wife Over 35 yrs. | Wife Under 35 yrs. | Total | Wife Over 35 yrs. | Wife Under 35 yrs. | Total |
|---|---|---|---|---|---|---|
| Nuclear | 659 | 960 | 1619 | 64.0 | 74.8 | 70.0 |
| Joint | 371 | 324 | 695 | 36.0 | 25.2 | 30.0 |
| Total | 1030 | 1284 | 2314 | 100.0 | 100.0 | 100.0 |

married primary kin with whom they could form a joint-family. But this does not really explain the difference. When only couples having a choice between the nuclear and joint-family are considered (eligibles), one finds that the variation between old and young couples in their actual incidence of joint-family living clearly indicates the difference in their preference for this form. Whereas 48.1 per cent of the eligibles among the old couples chose the joint-family, only 36.8 per cent of those among the young couples did so (Table 20). In

TABLE 19
Number and Percentage of Couples Having Married, Primary Kin (Eligibles) by Age of Wife

| MARRIED PRIMARY KIN | NUMBER | | | PERCENTAGE | | |
| | Wife Over 35 yrs. | Wife Under 35 yrs. | Total | Wife Over 35 yrs. | Wife Under 35 yrs. | Total |
|---|---|---|---|---|---|---|
| Some (Eligibles) | 772 | 889 | 1661 | 74.9 | 69.2 | 71.9 |
| None (Ineligibles) | 258 | 395 | 653 | 25.1 | 30.8 | 28.1 |
| Total | 1030 | 1284 | 2314 | 100.0 | 100.0 | 100.0 |

effect, the joint-family is both more frequent among and more preferred by the old couples.

TABLE 20
Number and Percentage of Eligible Couples Having Joint Family, by Age of Wife

| FAMILY STRUCTURE | NUMBER | | | PERCENTAGE | | |
| | Wife Over 35 yrs. | Wife Under 35 yrs. | Total | Wife Over 35 yrs. | Wife Under 35 yrs. | Total |
| --- | --- | --- | --- | --- | --- | --- |
| Nuclear | 401 | 565 | 966 | 51.9 | 63.2 | 58.2 |
| Joint | 371 | 324 | 695 | 48.1 | 36.8 | 41.8 |
| Total | 772 | 889 | 1661 | 100.0 | 100.0 | 100.0 |

*RESIDENCE AND FAMILY STRUCTURE*

Residential groups differ in their frequency of and preference for joint-family living. According to column 5 of Table 21, the percentage of couples having this family form is 37.0 in the villages but only 24.9 in the towns and 22.9 in the city. Actual family structure is a

TABLE 21
Number and Percentage of Total Couples and Eligible Couples Having Joint Family, by Residence

| RESIDENCE (1) | NUMBER OF COUPLES | | | JOINT FAMILY AS PERCENTAGE OF | |
| | Total (2) | Having Primary Kin (Eligibles) (3) | Having Joint Family (4) | Total Couples (5) | Eligible Couples (6) |
| --- | --- | --- | --- | --- | --- |
| City | 882 | 627 | 202 | 22.9 | 32.2 |
| Town | 309 | 195 | 77 | 24.9 | 39.5 |
| Village | 1123 | 839 | 416 | 37.0 | 49.6 |
| Total | 2314 | 1661 | 695 | 30.0 | 41.8 |

fair index of differences among residential groups in their preference for joint-family living. When only couples which had a choice between living in a nuclear family or a joint-family are considered, one finds, in column 6, that 49.6 per cent of the villagers, 39.5 per

**43**

cent of the town dwellers, and 32.2 per cent of the city dwellers chose to live in a joint-family.

Comparison of columns 4 and 7 of Table 22 indicates that the tendency to live "jointly" is stronger among the old couples than the

TABLE 22
Number and Percentage of Couples Having a Joint Family by Age of Wife and Residence

| Residence | *Wife Over 35 Years* | | | *Wife Under 35 Years* | | |
| | TOTAL | JOINT FAMILY | | TOTAL | JOINT FAMILY | |
| | Number | Number | Percentage | Number | Number | Percentage |
| (1) | (2) | (3) | (4) | (5) | (6) | (7) |
| City | 401 | 115 | *28.7* | 481 | 87 | *18.1* |
| Town | 124 | 39 | *30.6* | 185 | 38 | *20.5* |
| Village | 505 | 217 | *43.0* | 618 | 199 | *32.2* |
| Total | 1030 | 371 | 36.0 | 1284 | 324 | 25.2 |

TABLE 23
Number and Percentage of Total Couples and Eligible Couples Having Joint Family, by Religion

| | NUMBER OF COUPLES | | | JOINT FAMILY AS | |
| | | Having | Having | PERCENTAGE OF | |
| | | Primary Kin | Joint | Total | Eligible |
| RELIGION | Total | (Eligibles) | Family | Couples | Couples |
| (1) | (2) | (3) | (4) | (5) | (6) |
| Hindu | 1923 | 1371 | 604 | 31.4 | 44.2 |
| Buddhist | 237 | 182 | 56 | 23.6 | 30.8 |
| Muslim | 97 | 67 | 28 | 28.9 | 41.8 |
| Other | 57 | 41 | 7 | 12.3 | 17.1 |
| Total | 2314 | 1661 | 695 | 30.0 | 41.8 |

young couples in all three residential areas. The percentages of old and young couples living "jointly" are, respectively, 28.7 and 18.1 in the city, 30.6 and 20.5 in the towns, and 43.0 and 32.2 in the villages.

*RELIGION, CASTE, AND FAMILY STRUCTURE*

Among religious groups, as might be expected, the joint-family is more frequent among Hindus than among Buddhists, Muslims, and

44

persons of "Other Religion" (Christians, Parsees, Sikhs, and Jains). Most striking is the fact that only 12.3 per cent of those of "Other Religion" lived jointly as compared with 31.4 per cent of the Hindus. The percentages are 23.6 for Buddhists and 28.9 for Muslims. The actual prevalence of joint-families among religious groups reflects differences among them in their preference for joint-family living. According to column 6 of Table 23, of the couples who had a choice between living separately from or jointly with their married primary kinsmen, 44.2 per cent of the Hindus, 30.8 per cent of the Buddhists, 41.8 per cent of the Muslims, and 17.1 per cent of those of "Other Religion" chose to live jointly.

Comparison of old and young couples indicates that joint-family living has declined[23] among Hindus, Buddhists, and Muslims. The percentage having a joint family drops from: 38.3 to 25.8 for Hindus; 31.8 to 26.4 for Muslims; and from 27.3 to 21.0 for Buddhists. In the case of couples of "Other Religion," it rises from 3.4 per cent to 21.4 per cent.

When Hindus are differentiated by caste affiliation, considerable variation in the prevalence of joint-family living is evident. According to Table 25, the percentage having this living arrangement is high among the Telis (43.4), Kunbis (38.5), and Mahars (36.9), and is low

---

[23] It is important to note that differences between age groups in their prevalence of joint-families may not really reflect a trend. The assigning of this meaning to the data would be proper if family structure were static rather than dynamic during the lifetime of most couples. The usual pattern is for couples to experience a cycle of family structures (nuclear family, extended nuclear family, small joint-family, and large joint-family) because of the death of older kin, the marriage of younger kin, and the movement of kin of all ages into and out of the household for various economic and social reasons. It is not yet known whether particular phases of this cycle are more likely to occur as couples become older. But, if this should be the case, then it might account for the higher prevalence of joint-families among older couples. For a discussion of the general cyclical nature of family structure in India, see: A. Ross, *The Hindu Family in Its Urban Setting*, Toronto: University of Toronto Press, 1961, pp. 36–37; and S. C. Dube, *Indian Village*, London: Routledge and Kegan Paul, Ltd., 1955, pp. 132–135.

The most adequate procedure for ascertaining a trend in family structure is to compare the prevalence of joint-families among couples who are similar in age but who differ in decade of marriage. As we noted on page 38, the use of this procedure by Kapadia indicates that a slight decline in joint-families has occurred during the past twenty years.

TABLE 24
Number and Percentage of Couples Having a Joint Family by Age of Wife and Religion

| | Wife Over 35 Years | | | Wife Under 35 Years | | |
| | TOTAL | JOINT FAMILY | | TOTAL | JOINT FAMILY | |
| Religion | Number | Number | Percentage | Number | Number | Percentage |
| (1) | (2) | (3) | (4) | (5) | (6) | (7) |
|---|---|---|---|---|---|---|
| Hindu | 858 | 329 | 38.3 | 1065 | 275 | 25.8 |
| Buddhist | 99 | 27 | 27.3 | 138 | 29 | 21.0 |
| Muslim | 44 | 14 | 31.8 | 53 | 14 | 26.4 |
| Other | 29 | 1 | 3.4 | 28 | 6 | 21.4 |
| Total | 1030 | 371 | 36.0 | 1284 | 324 | 25.2 |

TABLE 25
Number and Percentage of Total Couples and Eligible Couples Having Joint Family, by Caste

| | NUMBER OF COUPLES | | | JOINT FAMILY AS PERCENTAGE OF | |
| | | Having Primary Kin | Having Joint | Total | Eligible |
| CASTE* | Total | (Eligibles) | Family | Couples | Couples |
| (1) | (2) | (3) | (4) | (5) | (6) |
|---|---|---|---|---|---|
| Brahmin | 215 | 161 | 33 | 15.3 | 20.5 |
| Maratha | 57 | 34 | 11 | 19.3 | 32.4 |
| Kunbi | 400 | 278 | 154 | 38.5 | 55.4 |
| Mali | 124 | 67 | 41 | 34.1 | 61.2 |
| Bania & other trading castes | 82 | 63 | 21 | 25.6 | 33.3 |
| Kosthi | 158 | 110 | 51 | 32.3 | 46.4 |
| Sonar & other artisan castes | 118 | 83 | 35 | 29.7 | 42.2 |
| Teli | 212 | 164 | 92 | 43.4 | 56.1 |
| Dhobi, nai & other service castes | 141 | 101 | 42 | 30.0 | 42.0 |
| Scheduled (Mahar | 130 | 93 | 48 | 36.9 | 51.6 |
| castes \Other | 68 | 50 | 19 | 28.0 | 38.0 |
| Gond | 50 | 43 | 16 | 32.0 | 37.2 |
| Other | 168 | 124 | 41 | 24.4 | 33.2 |
| Total Hindus | 1923 | 1371 | 604 | 31.4 | 44.2 |

* The specific castes included under Trading Castes, Artisan Castes, Service Castes, Scheduled Castes, and Other Castes are presented in Appendix I.

among the Brahmins (15.3), Marathas (19.3), and Trading Castes (25.6). The low figure for Brahmins is especially striking because they are ordinarily viewed as the preservers of traditional forms. Their preference for joint-family living is also relatively weak (column 6). Altogether 161 or 74.9 per cent of them had a choice between living separately from or jointly with kinsmen, but of these only 20.5 per cent chose to live jointly. The percentage preferring the joint-family is also low among the Marathas (32.4), Trading Castes (33.3), and Gonds (37.2). On the other hand, it was preferred by 61.2 per cent of the Malis, 56.1 per cent of the Telis, and 55.4 per cent of the Kunbis. As in the case of residential and religious groups, differences among castes in their actual frequency of joint-family living are therefore attributable to variations among them in their preference for this type of living rather than variations in the opportunity to live jointly.

BLE 26

mber and Percentage of Couples Having a Joint Family by Age
Wife and Caste

| Caste (1) | Wife Over 35 Years | | | Wife Under 35 Years | | |
|---|---|---|---|---|---|---|
| | TOTAL Number (2) | JOINT FAMILY Number (3) | Percentage (4) | TOTAL Number (5) | JOINT FAMILY Number (6) | Percentage (7) |
| hmin | 102 | 25 | 24.5 | 113 | 8 | 7.1 |
| ratha | 19 | 6 | 31.6 | 38 | 5 | 13.2 |
| nbi | 171 | 74 | 43.3 | 229 | 80 | 34.9 |
| li | 46 | 16 | 34.8 | 78 | 25 | 32.0 |
| ia and other ading castes | 42 | 11 | 26.2 | 40 | 10 | 25.0 |
| sthi | 75 | 32 | 42.7 | 83 | 19 | 22.9 |
| ar and other rtisan castes | 60 | 24 | 40.0 | 58 | 11 | 19.0 |
| | 96 | 47 | 48.9 | 116 | 45 | 38.8 |
| obi, nai & other ervice castes | 56 | 20 | 37.5 | 85 | 21 | 24.9 |
| eduled ∤Mahar astes ∖Other | 67 | 30 | 44.8 | 63 | 18 | 28.6 |
| | 28 | 11 | 39.2 | 40 | 8 | 20.0 |
| nd | 25 | 9 | 36.0 | 25 | 7 | 28.0 |
| er | 71 | 24 | 32.4 | 97 | 18 | 18.6 |
| otal Hindus | 858 | 329 | 38.3 | 1065 | 275 | 25.8 |

47

Comparison of the old and young couples shows that the frequency of joint-family living has declined in each caste. The declines, as columns 4 and 7 of Table 26 indicate, are very marked except in the case of Malis and Trading Castes where the percentage drops slightly from 34.8 to 32.0 and from 26.2 to 25.0, respectively. The greatest variations between old and young couples are present among the Brahmins (24.5 per cent and 7.1 per cent), Marathas (31.6 per cent and 13.2 per cent), and the Artisan Castes (40.0 per cent and 19.0 per cent).

### OCCUPATION AND FAMILY STRUCTURE

Variations in the frequency of joint-families are also evident when couples are differentiated on the basis of the husband's occupation. According to column 5 of Table 27, there is a vivid contrast between agriculturalists and clerical workers, the percentage of joint-families being 40.1 for the former but only 16.2 for the latter. Next to the agriculturalists are the traders (32.8 per cent), and then the artisans (28.8 per cent), unskilled workers (27.2 per cent), and, lastly, the

TABLE 27

Number and Percentage of Total Couples and Eligible Couples Having Joint Family, by Occupation of Husband*

| | NUMBER OF COUPLES | | | JOINT FAMILY AS PERCENTAGE OF | |
| OCCUPATIONAL GROUP** (1) | Total (2) | Having Primary Kin (Eligibles) (3) | Having Joint Family (4) | Total Couples (5) | Eligible Couples (6) |
| --- | --- | --- | --- | --- | --- |
| Unskilled | 272 | 199 | 74 | 27.2 | 37.2 |
| Artisan | 629 | 442 | 181 | 28.8 | 41.1 |
| Trade | 326 | 245 | 107 | 32.8 | 43.7 |
| Clerical | 198 | 140 | 32 | 16.2 | 22.9 |
| Professional and Administrative | 249 | 178 | 44 | 17.7 | 24.7 |
| Agricultural | 611 | 438 | 245 | 40.1 | 55.9 |
| Total | 2285 | 1642 | 683 | 30.0 | 41.8 |

\* Excludes 29 couples where the husband was unemployed.
\*\* The specific occupations included in each group are presented in Appendix II.

professionals (17.7 per cent). Insofar as preference is concerned, the groups differ in a similar manner. Joint-family living rather than nuclear family living was chosen by over half of the eligibles among agriculturalists, approximately forty per cent of those among the traders, artisans, and unskilled workers, and roughly a quarter of those among clerical and professional workers.

When old and young couples are compared (Table 28), one observes a marked decline in joint-family living in each occupational

TABLE 28

Number and Percentage of Couples Having a Joint Family by Age of Wife and Occupation of Husband*

| Occupational Group (1) | Wife Over 35 Years | | | Wife Under 35 Years | | |
|---|---|---|---|---|---|---|
| | TOTAL Number (2) | JOINT FAMILY | | TOTAL Number (5) | JOINT FAMILY | |
| | | Number (3) | Percentage (4) | | Number (6) | Percentage (7) |
| Unskilled | 112 | 41 | 36.6 | 160 | 33 | 20.6 |
| Artisan | 261 | 87 | 33.3 | 368 | 94 | 25.5 |
| Trade | 142 | 53 | 37.3 | 184 | 54 | 29.3 |
| Clerical | 68 | 16 | 23.5 | 130 | 16 | 12.3 |
| Professional and Admin. | 119 | 26 | 21.0 | 130 | 18 | 13.9 |
| Agricultural | 315 | 143 | 45.4 | 296 | 102 | 34.5 |
| Total | 1017 | 366 | 36.0 | 1268 | 317 | 25.2 |

* Excludes 29 couples where the husband was unemployed.

TABLE 29

Number and Percentage of Total Couples and Eligible Couples Having Joint Family, by Employment of Wife

| EMPLOYMENT STATUS OF WIFE (1) | NUMBER OF COUPLES | | | JOINT FAMILY AS PERCENTAGE OF | |
|---|---|---|---|---|---|
| | Total (2) | Having Primary Kin (Eligibles) (3) | Having Joint Family (4) | Total Couples (5) | Eligible Couples (6) |
| Unemployed | 2035 | 1479 | 626 | 30.8 | 42.3 |
| Employed | 279 | 182 | 69 | 24.7 | 37.9 |
| Total | 2314 | 1661 | 695 | 30.0 | 41.8 |

category. The decline is greatest in the clerical group, from 23.5 per cent to 12.3 per cent, and is least among the agriculturalists, from 45.4 per cent to 34.5 per cent.

The groups which result when couples are classified by the employment status of the wife rather than by the occupation of the husband vary in their prevalence of and preference for joint-family living. The percentage of joint-family structures is 30.8 for the unemployed and 24.7 for the employed, i.e., women earnings wages. Joint-family living was preferred by 42.3 per cent of the unemployed and 37.9 per cent of the employed. Again, one observes by Table 30 that the actual frequency of joint-families is greater among old couples than young couples in each category.

TABLE 30
Number and Percentage of Couples Having Joint Family by Age and Employment of Wife

| Employment Status of Wife (1) | Wife Over 35 Years | | | Wife Under 35 Years | | |
|---|---|---|---|---|---|---|
| | TOTAL Number (2) | JOINT Number (3) | FAMILY Percentage (4) | TOTAL Number (5) | JOINT Number (6) | FAMILY Percentag (7) |
| Unemployed | 883 | 326 | 37.0 | 1152 | 300 | 26.0 |
| Employed | 147 | 45 | 30.6 | 132 | 24 | 18.2 |
| Total | 1030 | 371 | 36.0 | 1284 | 324 | 25.2 |

*INCOME, LAND OWNERSHIP, AND FAMILY STRUCTURE*

The frequency of joint-families among income levels is presented in Table 31. It occurs most often in the lowest income group, those earning less than 500 rupees per year, and least often in the highest income group, those earning over 2000 rupees per year. There is not, however, a regular decrease in joint-families as income rises. Further, the variation in joint-families is quite small, the range being from 32.6 per cent to 23.8 per cent. Insofar as preference is concerned, by column 6, it declines regularly but not uniformly as income rises. Of those who had a choice between living separately from or jointly with primary kinsmen, 46.3 per cent of the lowest income group and 31.7 per cent of the highest group chose to live jointly.

TABLE 31

Number and Percentage of Total Couples and Eligible Couples Having Joint Family, by Income of Husband

| ANNUAL INCOME (IN RUPEES) (1) | NUMBER OF COUPLES | | | JOINT FAMILY AS PERCENTAGE OF | |
|---|---|---|---|---|---|
| | Total (2) | Having Primary Kin (Eligibles) (3) | Having Joint Family (4) | Total Couples (5) | Eligible Couples (6) |
| Under 500 | 650 | 458 | 212 | 32.6 | 46.3 |
| 500–999 | 877 | 622 | 266 | 30.3 | 42.8 |
| 1000–1499 | 360 | 263 | 111 | 30.8 | 42.2 |
| 1500–1999 | 124 | 91 | 34 | 27.4 | 37.4 |
| Over 2000 | 303 | 227 | 72 | 23.8 | 31.7 |
| Total | 2314 | 1661 | 695 | 30.0 | 41.8 |

According to columns 4 and 7 of Table 32, the frequency of joint-families has declined in every category. The decline is relatively small for the two lower income groups and large for the highest income group, where the percentage drops from 33.1 to 16.5.

TABLE 32

Number and Percentage of Couples Having a Joint Family by Age Wife and Income of Husband

| Annual Income (in rupees) (1) | Wife Over 35 Years | | | Wife Under 35 Years | | |
|---|---|---|---|---|---|---|
| | TOTAL Number (2) | JOINT FAMILY Number (3) | Percentage (4) | TOTAL Number (5) | JOINT FAMILY Number (6) | Percentage (7) |
| Under 500 | 286 | 108 | 37.7 | 364 | 104 | 28.6 |
| 500–999 | 378 | 135 | 35.7 | 499 | 131 | 26.3 |
| 1000–1499 | 173 | 66 | 38.1 | 187 | 45 | 24.1 |
| 1500–1999 | 42 | 15 | 35.7 | 82 | 19 | 23.2 |
| Over 2000 | 151 | 47 | 33.1 | 152 | 25 | 16.5 |
| Total | 1030 | 371 | 36.0 | 1284 | 324 | 25.2 |

When economic status is measured by the number of acres of land owned, one finds that the joint-family is most frequent among persons of medium status. According to column 5 of Table 33, the percentage having a joint-family is 27.1 for the landless, 27.0 for the small owners (1–9 acres), 40.1 for the medium owners (10–19 acres),

TABLE 33

Number and Percentage of Total Couples and Eligible Couples Having Joint Family, by Land Ownership

| LAND OWNERSHIP (IN ACRES) (1) | NUMBER OF COUPLES | | | JOINT FAMILY AS PERCENTAGE OF | |
| | Total (2) | Having Primary Kin (Eligibles) (3) | Having Joint Family (4) | Total Couples (5) | Eligible Couples (6) |
|---|---|---|---|---|---|
| None | 1308 | 928 | 355 | 27.1 | 38.3 |
| 1–9 | 403 | 268 | 109 | 27.0 | 40.7 |
| 10–19 | 297 | 227 | 119 | 40.1 | 52.4 |
| 20 & over | 306 | 238 | 112 | 36.6 | 47.1 |
| Total | 2314 | 1661 | 695 | 30.0 | 41.8 |

and 36.6 for the large owners. Preference for joint-family living is distributed in like manner. According to column 6, the percentage of eligibles choosing this living arrangement is 38.3 for the landless, 40.7 for the small owners, 52.4 for the medium owners, and 47.1 for the large owners.

Comparison of old and young couples shows that joint-family living has declined in each group. According to Table 34, the decline is greatest among small owners, from 33.3 per cent to 22.3 per cent, and is least among large owners, from 43.9 per cent to 35.6 per cent.

TABLE 34

Number and Percentage of Couples Having a Joint Family by Age of Wife and Land Ownership

| Land Ownership (in acres) (1) | Wife Over 35 Years | | | Wife Under 35 Years | | |
| | TOTAL Number (2) | JOINT FAMILY Number (2) | Percentage (4) | TOTAL Number (5) | JOINT FAMILY Number (6) | Percentage (7) |
|---|---|---|---|---|---|---|
| None | 547 | 176 | 32.2 | 761 | 169 | 22.2 |
| 1–9 | 174 | 58 | 33.3 | 229 | 51 | 22.3 |
| 10–19 | 152 | 68 | 44.7 | 145 | 51 | 35.2 |
| 20 & over | 157 | 69 | 43.9 | 149 | 53 | 35.6 |
| Total | 1030 | 371 | 36.0 | 1284 | 324 | 25.2 |

## EDUCATIONAL STATUS AND FAMILY STRUCTURE

The prevalence of joint-families among couples differentiated by the educational level of the male is presented in Table 35. As column 5 shows, there is a negative association between joint-family living and the level of education. The percentage having this arrangement is 36.3 for illiterates, 30.8 for primary educates, 30.5 for middle educates, 19.8 for non-matriculates, 14.3 for matriculates, and 9.2 for college educated. The preference for joint-family living is similarly distributed. According to column 6, the percentage of eligibles choosing the joint-family declines regularly but not uniformly from 48.5 in the illiterate group to 12.1 in the college group.

TABLE 35

Number and Percentage of Total Couples and Eligible Couples Having Joint Family, by Education of Husband

| EDUCATIONAL LEVEL OF HUSBAND (1) | NUMBER OF COUPLES | | | JOINT FAMILY AS PERCENTAGE OF | |
|---|---|---|---|---|---|
| | Total (2) | Having Primary Kin (Eligibles) (3) | Having Joint Family (4) | Total Couples (5) | Eligible Couples (6) |
| None | 891 | 667 | 323 | 36.3 | 48.5 |
| Primary | 736 | 510 | 227 | 30.8 | 44.5 |
| Middle | 302 | 212 | 92 | 30.5 | 43.3 |
| High | 86 | 57 | 17 | 19.8 | 29.8 |
| Matriculation | 168 | 116 | 24 | 14.3 | 20.7 |
| College | 131 | 99 | 12 | 9.2 | 12.1 |
| Total | 2314 | 1661 | 695 | 30.0 | 41.8 |

According to Table 36, the frequency of joint-family living has declined appreciably in all educational groups except the middle school group. The declines are rather uniform, being: 42.3 per cent to 29.1 per cent for illiterates; 38.2 per cent to 26.6 per cent for primary educates; 25.7 per cent to 15.7 per cent for non-matriculates; 18.1 per cent to 11.5 per cent for matriculates; and 11.5 per cent to 7.6 per cent for collegiates. In the case of those with middle schooling, the change is hardly perceptible, being from 30.1 per cent to 30.7 per cent.

When couples are differentiated on the basis of the wife's education, one observes again a decline in the frequency of joint-families as

53

## TABLE 36
Number and Percentage of Couples Having a Joint Family by Age
of Wife and Education of Husband

| Educational Level of Husband (1) | Wife Over 35 Years | | | Wife Under 35 Years | | |
|---|---|---|---|---|---|---|
| | TOTAL Number (2) | JOINT FAMILY Number (3) | JOINT FAMILY Percentage (4) | TOTAL Number (5) | JOINT FAMILY Number (6) | JOINT FAMILY Percenta (7) |
| None | 485 | 205 | 42.3 | 406 | 118 | 29.1 |
| Primary | 270 | 103 | 38.2 | 466 | 124 | 26.6 |
| Middle | 116 | 35 | 30.1 | 186 | 57 | 30.7 |
| High | 35 | 9 | 25.7 | 51 | 8 | 15.7 |
| Matriculation | 72 | 13 | 18.1 | 96 | 11 | 11.5 |
| College | 52 | 6 | 11.5 | 79 | 6 | 7.6 |
| Total | 1030 | 371 | 36.0 | 1284 | 324 | 25.2 |

## TABLE 37
Number and Percentage of Total Couples and Eligible Couples
Having Joint Family, by Education of Wife

| EDUCATIONAL LEVEL OF WIFE (1) | NUMBER OF COUPLES | | | JOINT FAMILY AS PERCENTAGE OF | |
|---|---|---|---|---|---|
| | Total (2) | Having Primary Kin (Eligibles) (3) | Having Joint Family (4) | Total Couples (5) | Eligible Couples (6) |
| None | 1772 | 1290 | 598 | 33.8 | 46.4 |
| Primary | 318 | 213 | 68 | 21.4 | 31.9 |
| Above Primary | 224 | 158 | 29 | 13.0 | 18.4 |
| Total | 2314 | 1661 | 695 | 30.0 | 41.8 |

## TABLE 38
Number and Percentage of Couples Having a Joint Family by Age
and Education of Wife

| Educational Level of Wife (1) | Wife Over 35 Years | | | Wife Under 35 Years | | |
|---|---|---|---|---|---|---|
| | TOTAL Number (2) | JOINT FAMILY Number (3) | JOINT FAMILY Percentage (4) | TOTAL Number (5) | JOINT FAMILY Number (6) | JOINT FAMILY Percenta (7) |
| None | 858 | 341 | 39.7 | 914 | 257 | 28.1 |
| Primary | 99 | 20 | 20.1 | 219 | 48 | 21.9 |
| Above Primary | 73 | 10 | 13.7 | 151 | 19 | 12.6 |
| Total | 1030 | 371 | 36.0 | 1284 | 324 | 25.2 |

54

education increases. According to Table 37, the percentage having a joint-family is 33.8 for illiterates, 21.4 for those with primary schooling, and 13.0 for those having more than primary schooling. Of those who had a choice between living separately from or jointly with their primary kinsmen, one observes by column 6 that 46.4 per cent of the illiterates, 31.9 per cent of the primary educates, and 18.4 per cent of the higher educates chose to live jointly.

These groups, unlike most others, do not show regular patterns of decline in joint-family living. The percentages of old and young couples living jointly are, respectively, 39.7 and 28.1 for illiterates, 20.1 and 21.9 for primary educates, and 13.7 and 12.6 for those of higher education. In effect, the only significant decline occurs among the illiterates.

## SUMMARY

Our review of the writings of various authorities on the family indicates that little is known about the prevalence of joint-families in areas of India other than Gujerat and Saurashtra. There is likewise little information on the actual effect of joint-family living on the fertility of couples, but two kinds of influence are presumed to operate. According to one set of writers, the joint-family tends to keep fertility below the level that it would reach if a couple lived separately from its kinsmen, i.e., in a nuclear family. This depressant action presumably stems from the limited amount of sexual intercourse which couples are permitted because of a lack of privacy and the controls over conduct which elders exert. According to the other school of thought, the joint-family encourages high fertility by stressing the economic, political, and social benefits which accrue to couples having a large number of children.

According to our data on Central India, the joint-family occurs less frequently here than in Gujerat or Saurashtra. Its prevalence is especially low in the city and towns, and among couples who belong to the minority religions. Within the Hindu group, Telis and Kunbis frequently have joint-families whereas Brahmins and Marathas rarely have them. This family form is also rare among couples who belong to the clerical and professional occupations as well as those who have high earnings and who have attained more than secondary school education. Lastly, according to our comparisons of old and young couples, it seems that both the prevalence of and preference for joint-family living has declined in Central India.

The analyses performed in this chapter will permit us in Chapter Five to determine whether the frequency of joint-families is related to the fertility averages of various socio-economic strata.

# Age at Marriage and Socio-economic Status

AGE at marriage is another cultural factor which may account for differences among socio-economic strata in fertility performance. It is therefore the purpose of this chapter to describe the ages at which husbands and wives in the several strata usually marry. These findings will permit us in subsequent chapters to determine whether fertility differentials are, in fact, explained by variations in age at marriage. If the two variables—fertility and age at marriage—are associated, then the future course of fertility in Central India will largely depend on whether age at marriage remains constant or fluctuates over time. Consequently, the other purpose of this chapter is to determine whether young and old wives in each stratum differ in age at marriage. Although a trend is more easily ascertained by placing women in several categories based on present age, we have not been able to follow this procedure, except when wives are undifferentiated by socio-economic status, because of the smallness of our sample. Our findings are presented after a review of the few reports on age at marriage and its relation to fertility in India.

## PREVIOUS STUDIES

Previous studies indicate that the ages at which males and females usually marry have remained relatively constant for several decades.[1] On the basis of census data, Agarwala finds that the average age for females rose from 13.0 years to only 15.4 years between 1921 and 1951.[2] Similar findings are reported by the National Sample Survey in its comparison of husbands and wives in different marriage periods. Taking the extremes, those married before 1910 and those

[1] For a review of studies of age at marriage in small, select groups, see: K. M. Kapadia, *Marriage and Family in India*, Second Edition, Bombay: Oxford University Press, 1958, pp. 156–159.

[2] S. N. Agarwala, "The Age at Marriage in India," *Population Index*, April 1957, pp. 96–107.

married during 1946–1951, one observes, after adjusting for the mortality factor, that the increase in age at marriage averages: 2.4 years (14.0 years to 16.4 years) for urban wives; 1.7 years (12.9 years to 14.6 years) for rural wives; 1.4 years (21.6 years to 23.0 years) for urban husbands; and 0.8 year (19.4 years to 20.2 years) for rural husbands.[3]

The studies do not provide us with any clear-cut relationship between age at marriage and fertility. According to the Poona Survey, the fertility rate in the city is higher for women married before age 15 than for those married between 15 and 19 years of age, and those married after age 19. But there is a lack of association between age at marriage and fertility in the non-city areas of Poona.[4] The National Sample Survey finds that women married before age 15 are low in fertility at various marriage durations up to 22 years, but after 22 years of marriage there is little difference between them and other women in either the urban or rural area.[5] Lastly, on the basis of data obtained by the United Nations Demographic Survey of Mysore State, it is estimated that overall fertility would be reduced by roughly 15.0 per cent if no woman married before 18 years of age and if the fertility pattern after age 18 remained as it is at present.[6] In response to this observation, Coale and Hoover have suggested that a large scale postponement of marriage and first cohabitation until age 18 might have the effect of increasing fertility by reducing the incidence of reproductive impairment associated with births at too early age.[7]

## OUR FINDINGS

The age at marriage for the 2314 wives whose first marriage was unbroken at the time of our survey is quite similar to that found by

[3] A. D. Gupta, R. K. Sen, M. Majumdar, and S. N. Mitra, *The National Sample Survey, No. 7: Couples Fertility*, New Delhi: Department of Economic Affairs, Ministry of Finance: Government of India, 1955, p. 24.

[4] V. M. Dandekar and K. Dandekar, *Survey of Fertility and Mortality in Poona District*, Poona: Gokhale Institute of Policits and Economics, Publication No. 27, 1953, pp. 58, 99.

[5] A. D. Gupta *et al, op. cit.*, pp. 34–35, 38.

[6] C. Chandrasekharan, "India's Population Problem," Unpublished Paper presented at the Inaugural Conference of the United Nations Demographic Teaching and Research Centre, Bombay, on November 5, 1957, p. 9.

[7] A. J. Coale and E. M. Hoover, *Population Growth and Economic Development in Low-Income Countries*, Princeton: Princeton University Press, 1958, p. 49.

previous studies. As Table 39 shows, 38.8 per cent married before age 13 or puberty;[8] 56.5 per cent married before age 15; and 82.1 per cent married before age 18. For the entire group, the median age at marriage is 14.1 years. Husbands, as one would expect, married at a much later age, their median being 21.2 years. Only 8.7 per cent of them were less than 15 years old and only 23.4 per cent of

TABLE 39

Number and Percentage of Husbands and Wives by Age at Marriage

| AGE AT MARRIAGE | NUMBER | | PERCENTAGE | |
|---|---|---|---|---|
| | Husbands | Wives | Husbands | Wives |
| Under 13 | 128 | 897 | 5.5 | 38.8 |
| 13–14 | 75 | 409 | 3.2 | 17.7 |
| 15–17 | 339 | 593 | 14.7 | 25.6 |
| 18–19 | 353 | 178 | 15.3 | 7.6 |
| 20–24 | 857 | 196 | 37.0 | 8.5 |
| 25–29 | 354 | 29 | 15.3 | 1.3 |
| 30–34 | 111 | 9 | 4.8 | 0.4 |
| 35–39 | 41 | 3 | 1.8 | 0.1 |
| 40–44 | 30 | — | 1.3 | — |
| 45 and over | 26 | — | 1.1 | — |
| Total | 2314 | 2314 | 100.0 | 100.0 |

them were less than 18 years old at the time of marriage as compared with 56.5 per cent and 82.1 per cent of the wives. According to these data, it seems that some husbands and the majority of wives married before reaching the minimum age set by law.

According to the Child Marriage Restraint Act passed in 1929 in British India, the marriage of a male under 18 years of age or a female under 14 years of age is punishable by fine or imprisonment, or both.[9] In 1955, the Hindu Marriage Act raised the minimum for females to age 15.[10] When age at marriage is computed for only those persons married since the passage of the 1929 act, we find that 40.0 per cent

[8] A small scale inquiry conducted in Calcutta shows that the menarcheal age of Bengali girls varies from 12.74 years to 12.78 years; in the absence of other studies, it is not possible to know whether women in other parts of India reach puberty at this age. Source: K. M. Kapadia, *op. cit.*, p. 160.

[9] K. M. Kapadia, *op. cit.*, p. 154.

[10] *Ibid.*, p. 156.

of the wives and 16.2 per cent of the husbands were younger than the legal age. When these persons are grouped by periods of marriage (1930–1939, 1940–1949, and 1950–1957), there is a decline over time in the percentage of unlawful marriages. The percentages for the three periods are: 53.4, 37.9, and 19.5 for the wives; and 24.4, 16.2, and 4.5 for the husbands.

TABLE 40

Relation Between Husband and Wife in Age at Marriage

| HUSBAND'S AGE AT MARRIAGE (in years) | WIFE'S AGE AT MARRIAGE (IN YEARS) | | | | | | |
| --- | --- | --- | --- | --- | --- | --- | --- |
| | Under 10 | 10– 14 | 15– 19 | 20– 24 | 25– 29 | 30– 39 | TOTAL |
| Under 10 | 22 | — | — | — | – | – | 22 |
| 10–14 | 143 | 38 | — | — | – | – | 181 |
| 15–19 | 136 | 497 | 58 | 1 | – | – | 692 |
| 20–24 | 16 | 381 | 431 | 29 | – | – | 857 |
| 25–29 | 2 | 48 | 204 | 95 | 5 | – | 354 |
| 30–34 | — | 13 | 50 | 39 | 8 | 1 | 111 |
| 35–39 | — | 3 | 19 | 9 | 7 | 3 | 41 |
| 40–44 | 1 | 4 | 6 | 11 | 5 | 3 | 30 |
| 45 and over | 2 | — | 3 | 12 | 4 | 5 | 26 |
| Total | 322 | 984 | 771 | 196 | 29 | 12 | 2314 |
| Midpoint of Age Interval (Wives) | 7.5 | 12.5 | 17.5 | 22.5 | 27.5 | 35.0 | 14.1 |
| Median Age (Husbands) | 14.9 | 19.6 | 23.8 | 28.6 | 36.4 | 43.3 | 21.2 |
| Average Difference | 7.4 | 7.1 | 6.3 | 6.1 | 8.9 | 8.3 | 7.1 |

Although husbands and wives as groups differ considerably in age at marriage, there is not ordinarily a great discrepancy between an individual husband and his spouse in age at marriage. Six of the husbands were either slightly younger than or identical to their wives in age, and 93 were only one or two years older. In the remainder of the 2314 marriages, the husband was older by: three or four years in 342 cases; five or six years in 747 cases; seven or eight years in 469 cases; and by more than eighteen years in 79 cases. Large differences in age at marriage occur most frequently among couples who marry relatively late in life. As the last row of Table 40 shows, the average difference is 7.1 years for our entire series of marriages but it is over eight years for marriages which occurred after the woman reached 25 years of age.

When age at marriage is related to current age (over 45 years, 35–44 years, 25–34 years, and under 25 years), a slight rise in age at marriage is observable for both husbands and wives. The medians for husbands in the different age categories are: 19.8 years; 20.9 years; 22.1 years; and 22.4 years. For the wives they are: 12.9 years; 13.8 years; 14.8 years; and 15.3 years. If one assumes that those over 45 years of age and those under 25 years of age represent different

TABLE 41

Relation of Age at Marriage to Present Age of Wives

| Age at Marriage | Present Age | | | | | | | |
|---|---|---|---|---|---|---|---|---|
| | NUMBER | | | | PERCENTAGE | | | |
| | Over 45 | 35–44 | 25–34 | Under 25 | Over 45 | 35–44 | 25–34 | Under 25 |
| Under 13 | 235 | 247 | 263 | 152 | 50.4 | 43.8 | 33.8 | 30.0 |
| 13–17 | 156 | 225 | 347 | 274 | 33.5 | 39.9 | 44.6 | 54.2 |
| 18 and over | 75 | 92 | 168 | 80 | 16.1 | 16.3 | 21.6 | 15.8 |
| Total | 466 | 564 | 778 | 506 | 100.0 | 100.0 | 100.0 | 100.0 |

generations, then it may be said that the median age at marriage has, over a generation, risen by 2.6 years (19.8 to 22.4) for husbands and 2.4 years (12.9 to 15.3) for wives. The increase in the median for wives is primarily due to the fact that a smaller percentage of younger wives married before reaching puberty. According to Table 41, 50.4 per cent of the women over 45 years of age but only 30.0 per cent of those under 25 years of age married before age 13. Further, the percentage marrying between ages 13 and 17 increases as current age decreases but the percentage marrying after age 18 remains quite constant from one age group to the next.

*RESIDENCE AND AGE AT MARRIAGE*

Variations in age at marriage are evident when couples are differentiated by place of residence. City wives marry, on the average, at 15.5 years of age whereas those in the towns and villages marry at 13.6 years and 13.4 years of age, respectively. The averages for

TABLE 42
Age at Marriage of Husbands and Wives by Residence

| | Number of Couples | Age at Marriage (in years) | | |
| | | MEDIANS | | DIFFERENCE IN MEDIANS |
| Residence | | Husbands | Wives | |
|---|---|---|---|---|
| City | 882 | 22.5 | 15.5 | 7.0 |
| Town | 309 | 21.0 | 13.6 | 7.4 |
| Village | 1123 | 20.3 | 13.4 | 6.9 |
| Total | 2314 | 21.2 | 14.1 | 7.1 |

husbands are 22.5 years in the city, 21.0 years in the towns, and 20.3 years in the villages. As Table 42 shows, the husband-wife difference in age at marriage is roughly the same in all three areas.

Comparison of wives over 35 years of age with those under 35 years of age reveals a rise in age at marriage in all three areas. It is relatively insignificant in the city (0.7 year) but considerable in the towns (1.6 years) and villages (2.0 years).

TABLE 43
Median Age at Marriage of Wives Over and Under 35 Years of Age, by Residence

| | NUMBER | | MEDIAN AGE AT MARRIAGE | | INCREASE IN MEDIAN |
| RESIDENCE | Over 35 | Under 35 | Over 35 | Under 35 | |
|---|---|---|---|---|---|
| City | 401 | 481 | 14.9 | 15.6 | 0.7 |
| Town | 124 | 185 | 12.5 | 14.1 | 1.6 |
| Village | 505 | 618 | 12.1 | 14.1 | 2.0 |
| Total | 1030 | 1284 | 13.4 | 15.0 | 1.6 |

*RELIGION, CASTE, AND AGE AT MARRIAGE*

There is considerable variation among religious groups in their ages at marriage. At one extreme are wives in the Hindu group with a median of 14.0 years and at the other extreme are wives in "Other religions" (Christians, Parsees, Sikhs, and Jains) with a median of 18.6 years. Among husbands, too, the greatest difference occurs

TABLE 44
Age at Marriage of Husbands and Wives, by Religion

| | | Age at Marriage (in years) | | |
| | Number | MEDIANS | | DIFFERENCE IN |
| Religion | of Couples | Husbands | Wives | MEDIANS |
|---|---|---|---|---|
| Hindu | 1923 | 21.0 | 14.0 | 7.0 |
| Buddhist | 237 | 21.2 | 14.5 | 6.7 |
| Muslim | 97 | 24.0 | 16.7 | 7.3 |
| Other | 57 | 26.6 | 18.6 | 8.0 |
| Total | 2314 | 21.2 | 14.1 | 7.1 |

between Hindus and those of "Other religions," their respective medians being 21.0 years and 26.6 years. The difference between husband and wife in age at marriage is, on the average, highest among "Other religions" (8.0 years) and lowest among Buddhists (6.7 years).

According to Table 45, the median age at marriage for wives has

TABLE 45
Median Age at Marriage of Wives Over and Under 35 Years of Age, by Religion

| | NUMBER | | MEDIAN AGE AT MARRIAGE | | INCREASE |
| RELIGION | Over 35 | Under 35 | Over 35 | Under 35 | IN MEDIAN |
|---|---|---|---|---|---|
| Hindu | 858 | 1065 | 12.9 | 14.7 | 1.8 |
| Buddhist | 99 | 138 | 14.2 | 14.7 | 0.5 |
| Muslim | 44 | 53 | 16.6 | 16.8 | 0.2 |
| Other | 29 | 28 | 19.7 | 16.9 | −2.8 |
| Total | 1030 | 1284 | 13.4 | 15.0 | 1.6 |

risen by 1.8 years for Hindus and by only 0.5 year for Buddhists. On the other hand, the median for Muslims has not changed whereas that for "Other religions" has actually declined by 2.8 years.

Age at marriage also varies among Hindus differentiated according to caste identity. The greatest differences exist between Brahmin and Maratha wives who have medians of 16.9 years and 16.0 years, and Kunbi and Teli wives who have medians of 12.7 years and 12.6 years.

63

Husbands in these castes likewise constitute the extremes in terms of age at marriage. One observes, too, in Table 46 that there are several castes whose wives have medians between 13.3 years and 13.5 years (Mali, Artisan Castes, Service Castes, Mahar, and Gond) and whose husbands have medians between 20.4 years and 20.9 years (Mali, Kosthi, Artisan Castes, Mahar, and Gond). Insofar as husband-wife

TABLE 46

Age at Marriage of Husbands and Wives, by Caste

| Caste | Number of Couples | Age at Marriage (in years) | | |
|---|---|---|---|---|
| | | MEDIANS | | DIFFERENCE IN MEDIANS |
| | | Husbands | Wives | |
| Brahmin | 215 | 24.9 | 16.9 | 8.0 |
| Maratha | 57 | 23.8 | 16.0 | 7.8 |
| Kunbi | 400 | 19.7 | 12.7 | 7.0 |
| Mali | 124 | 20.7 | 13.3 | 7.4 |
| Bania and other trading castes | 82 | 22.0 | 15.5 | 6.5 |
| Kosthi | 158 | 20.5 | 13.8 | 6.7 |
| Sonar and other artisan castes | 118 | 20.4 | 13.3 | 7.1 |
| Teli | 212 | 19.2 | 12.6 | 6.6 |
| Dhobi, nai and other service castes | 141 | 19.9 | 13.4 | 6.5 |
| Scheduled ⌠Mahar | 130 | 20.7 | 13.5 | 7.2 |
| castes ⌊Other | 68 | 21.0 | 14.1 | 6.9 |
| Gond | 50 | 20.9 | 13.5 | 7.4 |
| Other | 168 | 22.3 | 15.2 | 7.1 |
| Total Hindus | 1923 | 21.0 | 14.0 | 7.0 |

difference in age at marriage is concerned, it is greatest among Brahmins (8.0 years) and least among Trading Castes and Service Castes (6.5 years).

According to Table 47, the age of wives at marriage has increased in every caste group except the set of "Other" or miscellaneous castes. This increase is 2.2 years or more among Brahmins, Marathas, Mahars, and Gonds but less than a year in the case of Trading Castes, Service Castes, and Scheduled Castes (excluding Mahars).

TABLE 47

Median Age at Marriage of Wives Over and Under 35 Years of Age, by Caste

| | NUMBER | | MEDIAN AGE AT MARRIAGE | | INCREASE |
| | Over | Under | Over | Under | IN |
| CASTE | 35 | 35 | 35 | 35 | MEDIAN |
|---|---|---|---|---|---|
| Brahmin | 102 | 113 | 15.0 | 18.9 | 3.9 |
| Maratha | 19 | 38 | 13.9 | 16.7 | 2.8 |
| Kunbi | 171 | 229 | 11.8 | 13.4 | 1.6 |
| Mali | 46 | 78 | 12.2 | 13.9 | 1.7 |
| Bania and other trading castes | 42 | 40 | 15.2 | 15.8 | 0.6 |
| Kosthi | 75 | 83 | 12.7 | 14.3 | 1.6 |
| Sonar and other artisan castes | 60 | 58 | 12.8 | 14.2 | 1.4 |
| Teli | 96 | 116 | 11.9 | 13.7 | 1.8 |
| Dhobi, nai and other service castes | 56 | 85 | 13.0 | 13.7 | 0.7 |
| Scheduled ⎰Mahar | 67 | 63 | 12.4 | 15.1 | 2.7 |
| castes ⎱Other | 28 | 40 | 14.1 | 14.3 | 0.2 |
| Gond | 25 | 25 | 12.3 | 14.5 | 2.2 |
| Other | 71 | 97 | 15.2 | 15.2 | 0.0 |
| Total Hindus | 858 | 1065 | 12.9 | 14.7 | 1.8 |

TABLE 48

Age at Marriage of Husbands and Wives, by Occupation of Husband*

| | | Age at Marriage (in years) | | |
| | Number | | | DIFFERENCE |
| Occupational | of | MEDIANS | | IN |
| Group | Couples | Husbands | Wives | MEDIANS |
|---|---|---|---|---|
| Unskilled | 272 | 20.6 | 13.4 | 7.2 |
| Artisan | 629 | 20.6 | 13.7 | 6.9 |
| Trade | 326 | 22.1 | 15.1 | 7.0 |
| Clerical | 198 | 23.9 | 16.8 | 7.1 |
| Professional and Administrative | 249 | 24.1 | 16.2 | 7.9 |
| Agricultural | 611 | 19.0 | 13.0 | 6.0 |
| Total | 2285 | 21.2 | 14.1 | 7.1 |

* Excludes 29 couples where the husband was unemployed.

65

## OCCUPATION AND AGE AT MARRIAGE

When couples are classified by the husband's occupation, one finds that the median age at marriage for wives ranges from 13.0 years in the agricultural group to 16.8 years in the clerical group. In the case of husbands, agriculturalists have the lowest median, 19.0 years, and professionals have the highest median, 24.1 years. The difference between husband and wife in age at marriage is least, 6.0 years, among agriculturalists and greatest, 7.9 years, among professionals.

TABLE 49

Median Age at Marriage of Wives Over and Under 35 Years of Age, by Occupation of Husband*

|  | NUMBER | | MEDIAN AGE AT MARRIAGE | | INCREASE |
|  | Over 35 | Under 35 | Over 35 | Under 35 | IN MEDIAN |
| --- | --- | --- | --- | --- | --- |
| Unskilled | 112 | 160 | 12.5 | 14.7 | 2.2 |
| Artisan | 261 | 368 | 12.9 | 14.0 | 1.1 |
| Trade | 142 | 184 | 14.6 | 15.4 | 0.8 |
| Clerical | 68 | 130 | 15.3 | 17.6 | 2.3 |
| Professional and Admin. | 119 | 130 | 15.7 | 16.8 | 1.1 |
| Agricultural | 315 | 296 | 12.4 | 13.7 | 1.3 |
| Total | 1017 | 1268 | 13.4 | 15.0 | 1.6 |

* Excludes 29 women whose husbands were unemployed.

According to Table 49, age at marriage has increased for wives in all occupational strata. The increase ranges from 0.8 year for the trade group to 2.3 years for the clerical group and 2.2 years for the unskilled group. Those in the artisan, professional, and agricultural groups have increased by approximately 1.2 years.

The groups which result when couples are classified on the basis of the wife's employment status rather than husband's occupation also differ in age at marriage. According to Table 50, both husbands and wives in the unemployed group marry later than those in the employed group. The average difference between husband and wife in age at marriage is 7.1 years for the unemployed and 6.8 years for the

TABLE 50

Age at Marriage of Husbands and Wives, by Employment of Wife

| Employment Status of Wife | Number of Couples | Age at Marriage (in years) | | |
|---|---|---|---|---|
| | | MEDIANS | | DIFFERENCE IN MEDIANS |
| | | Husbands | Wives | |
| Unemployed | 2035 | 21.5 | 14.4 | 7.1 |
| Employed | 279 | 20.1 | 13.3 | 6.8 |
| Total | 2314 | 21.2 | 14.1 | 7.1 |

TABLE 51

Median Age at Marriage of Wives Over and Under 35 Years of Age, by Employment Status

| EMPLOYMENT STATUS OF WIFE | NUMBER | | MEDIAN AGE AT MARRIAGE | | INCREASE IN MEDIAN |
|---|---|---|---|---|---|
| | Over 35 | Under 35 | Over 35 | Under 35 | |
| Unemployed | 883 | 1152 | 13.5 | 15.0 | 1.5 |
| Employed | 147 | 132 | 13.0 | 13.6 | 0.6 |
| Total | 1030 | 1284 | 13.4 | 15.0 | 1.6 |

TABLE 52

Age at Marriage of Husbands and Wives, by Income of Husband

| Annual Income (in rupees) | Number of Couples | Age at Marriage (in years) | | |
|---|---|---|---|---|
| | | MEDIANS | | DIFFERENCE IN MEDIANS |
| | | Husbands | Wives | |
| Under 500 | 650 | 19.9 | 13.0 | 6.9 |
| 500–999 | 877 | 20.9 | 14.0 | 6.9 |
| 1000–1499 | 360 | 21.8 | 14.6 | 7.2 |
| 1500–1999 | 124 | 24.7 | 16.9 | 7.8 |
| 2000 and over | 303 | 24.0 | 16.6 | 7.4 |
| Total | 2314 | 21.2 | 14.1 | 7.1 |

employed. According to Table 51, the median age at marriage has risen by 1.5 years for unemployed wives and by 0.6 year for employed wives.

*INCOME, LAND OWNERSHIP, AND AGE AT MARRIAGE*

Table 52 presents the relationship of age at marriage to husband's annual income. Although age at marriage is not directly associated with increasing income, there is a tendency for those in the higher income categories to marry late. At the extremes are the medians of 13.0 years and 19.9 years for wives and husbands, respectively, in the Under 500 rupee group, and the medians of 16.9 years and 24.7 years for wives and husbands, respectively, in the 1500–1999 rupee group. Wives and husbands in the highest income group, 2000 rupees or more, have medians of 16.6 years and 24.0 years, respectively. The husband-wife difference in age at marriage is least—6.9 years—in the two lower income groups and is most—7.8 years—in the 1500–1999 rupee group.

According to Table 53, the median age of wives at marriage has remained constant in the 1500–1999 rupee category and has increased by only 0.5 year in the Under 500 rupee category. In the other three income categories, the increase approximates two years.

Among land ownership groups there is a small amount of variation in age at marriage. Wives of small owners (1–9 acres) and those of median owners (10–19 acres) have almost identical medians of 13.3 years and 13.2 years. Wives of the landless and those of large owners (20 acres and over) are likewise almost identical, having medians of 14.7 years and 14.5 years. As Table 54 shows, the same patterns are present among husbands in the different groups. Insofar as husband-wife difference in age at marriage is concerned, it is 6.7 years for the medium owners and just about 7.0 years for each of the other three groups.

According to Table 55, the age of wives at marriage has increased in every land ownership group. The increase is 1.2 years for those in the landless and medium ownership groups, 1.5 years for those in the small ownership group, and 1.8 years for those in the large ownership group.

TABLE 53

Median Age at Marriage of Wives Over and Under 35 Years of Age, by Income of Husband

| ANNUAL INCOME (IN RUPEES) | NUMBER | | MEDIAN AGE AT MARRIAGE | | INCREASE IN MEDIAN |
|---|---|---|---|---|---|
| | Over 35 | Under 35 | Over 35 | Under 35 | |
| Under 500 | 286 | 364 | 12.7 | 13.2 | 0.5 |
| 500–999 | 378 | 499 | 12.7 | 14.6 | 1.9 |
| 1000–1499 | 173 | 187 | 13.5 | 15.3 | 1.8 |
| 1500–1999 | 42 | 82 | 16.9 | 16.9 | 0.0 |
| 2000 and over | 151 | 152 | 15.4 | 17.5 | 2.1 |
| Total | 1030 | 1284 | 13.4 | 15.0 | 1.6 |

TABLE 54

Age at Marriage of Husbands and Wives, by Land Ownership

| Land Ownership (in acres) | Number of Couples | Age at Marriage (in years) | | DIFFERENCE IN MEDIANS |
|---|---|---|---|---|
| | | MEDIANS | | |
| | | Husbands | Wives | |
| None | 1308 | 21.8 | 14.7 | 7.1 |
| 1–9 | 403 | 20.3 | 13.3 | 7.0 |
| 10–19 | 297 | 19.9 | 13.2 | 6.7 |
| 20 and over | 306 | 21.5 | 14.5 | 7.0 |
| Total | 2314 | 21.2 | 14.1 | 7.1 |

TABLE 55

Median Age at Marriage of Wives Over and Under 35 Years of Age, by Land Ownership

| LAND OWNERSHIP (IN ACRES) | NUMBER | | MEDIAN AGE AT MARRIAGE | | INCREASE IN MEDIANS |
|---|---|---|---|---|---|
| | Over 35 | Under 35 | Over 35 | Under 35 | |
| None | 547 | 761 | 13.9 | 15.1 | 1.2 |
| 1–9 | 174 | 229 | 12.7 | 14.2 | 1.5 |
| 10–19 | 152 | 145 | 12.7 | 13.9 | 1.2 |
| 20 and over | 157 | 149 | 13.4 | 15.2 | 1.8 |
| Total | 1030 | 1284 | 13.4 | 15.0 | 1.6 |

*EDUCATION AND AGE AT MARRIAGE*

Table 56 shows that the age at marriage for both husbands and wives is directly associated with the husband's educational attainment. The medians range from 12.9 years for wives and 19.6 years for husbands in the illiterate group to 18.6 years for wives and 26.3 years for husbands in the college-educated group. The difference between husband and wife in age at marriage is least among illiterates—6.7 years—and is greatest among matriculates—8.1 years.

TABLE 56

Age at Marriage of Husbands and Wives, by Education of Husband

| Educational Level of Husband | Number of Couples | Age at Marriage (in years) | | DIFFERENCE IN MEDIANS |
|---|---|---|---|---|
| | | MEDIANS | | |
| | | Husbands | Wives | |
| None | 891 | 19.6 | 12.9 | 6.7 |
| Primary | 736 | 20.8 | 14.0 | 6.8 |
| Middle | 302 | 22.2 | 15.1 | 7.1 |
| High | 86 | 23.7 | 16.3 | 7.4 |
| Matriculation | 168 | 24.8 | 16.7 | 8.1 |
| College | 131 | 26.3 | 18.6 | 7.7 |
| Total | 2314 | 21.2 | 14.1 | 7.1 |

According to Table 57, the age of wives at marriage has remained constant for those whose husbands have middle or high school education. It has increased by 1.4 years for wives of illiterates, 1.8 years for wives of primary school educates, and by roughly 2.5 years for wives of matriculates and college educates.

When couples are classified by the wife's educational attainment, one observes in Table 58 that education and age at marriage are again associated. The medians are 13.4 years for illiterate wives, 15.8 years for those with primary schooling, and 18.4 years for those with more than primary schooling. The medians for their husbands are, respectively, 20.2 years, 23.6 years, and 26.0 years. The husband-wife difference in age at marriage is 6.8 years for the illiterate, 7.8 years for the primary educates, and 7.6 years for those with more than primary schooling.

70

TABLE 57

Median Age at Marriage of Wives Over and Under 35 Years of Age, by Education of Husband

| EDUCATIONAL LEVEL OF HUSBAND | NUMBER | | MEDIAN AGE AT MARRIAGE | | INCREASE IN MEDIAN |
|---|---|---|---|---|---|
| | Over 35 | Under 35 | Over 35 | Under 35 | |
| None | 485 | 406 | 12.4 | 13.7 | 1.4 |
| Primary | 270 | 466 | 12.6 | 14.4 | 1.8 |
| Middle | 116 | 186 | 15.1 | 15.1 | 0.0 |
| High | 35 | 51 | 16.3 | 16.3 | 0.0 |
| Matriculation | 72 | 96 | 15.4 | 17.9 | 2.5 |
| College | 52 | 79 | 17.0 | 19.4 | 2.4 |
| Total | 1030 | 1284 | 13.4 | 15.0 | 1.6 |

TABLE 58

Age at Marriage of Husbands and Wives, by Education of Wife

| Educational Level of Wife | Number of Couples | Age at Marriage (in years) | | DIFFERENCE IN MEDIANS |
|---|---|---|---|---|
| | | MEDIANS | | |
| | | Husbands | Wives | |
| None | 1772 | 20.2 | 13.4 | 6.8 |
| Primary | 318 | 23.6 | 15.8 | 7.8 |
| Above Primary | 224 | 26.0 | 18.4 | 7.6 |
| Total | 2314 | 21.2 | 14.1 | 7.1 |

TABLE 59

Median Age at Marriage of Wives Over and Under 35 Years of Age, by Education

| EDUCATIONAL LEVEL OF WIFE | NUMBER | | MEDIAN AGE AT MARRIAGE | | INCREASE IN MEDIAN |
|---|---|---|---|---|---|
| | Over 35 | Under 35 | Over 35 | Under 35 | |
| None | 858 | 914 | 12.8 | 14.0 | 1.2 |
| Primary | 99 | 219 | 15.7 | 15.8 | 0.1 |
| Above Primary | 73 | 151 | 18.0 | 18.6 | 0.6 |
| Total | 1030 | 1284 | 13.4 | 15.0 | 1.6 |

According to Table 59, the age of wives at marriage has remained constant for those with primary schooling, and has increased by 0.6 year for those with more than primary schooling, and by 1.2 years for those who are illiterate.

## SUMMARY

There are two general conclusions which can be derived from our review of the few reports on age at marriage and its relation to fertility in India. First, the ages at which males and females usually marry have remained rather constant over the past half-century. At present, the median ages at marriage are 16.4 years for urban women, 14.6 years for rural women, 23.0 years for urban men, and 20.2 years for rural men. Secondly, there is a positive association between early age at marriage and high fertility in certain regions but not in India as a whole.

According to our data, the median ages at marriage for women and men in Central India are slightly lower than the national averages. Early age at marriage is especially prominent in the villages, and among couples belonging to the Hindu and Buddhist faiths. Within the Hindu group, Telis and Kunbis frequently marry when young whereas Brahmins and Marathas seldom do so. The tendency to marry when quite young is also prominent among couples who belong to the agricultural and unskilled occupations as well as those who have low earnings and little or no formal education. As in other parts of India, age at marriage has risen very slightly among all socio-economic strata in Central India.

# Fertility Patterns and Socio-Economic Status

THIS chapter describes and compares the fertility patterns of various socio-economic strata, and measures the degree to which socio-economic differences in fertility are related to variations in either present age or age at marriage. Initially, it was planned to learn, too, whether differences among these strata in fertility can be attributed, in part or totally, to differences in either their marital composition, use of birth control techniques, or family structure. But, these analyses are now unnecessary. The first part of this chapter is concerned with general fertility patterns, and it clearly shows that none of these factors is related to fertility when women are not distinguished on the basis of socio-economic status. It would, therefore, be superfluous to go through the steps of analyzing their influence on the fertility performances of socio-economic strata.

## GENERAL PATTERNS

We noted in Chapter Two that our interviewers obtained complete information on the marital history and fertility of 2,469 living women. The total number of children ever born to them is 11,253 and the manner in which these births are distributed among the women results in a mean of 4.6 and a median of 4.7. As column 11 of Table 60 shows, there is a rather heavy concentration of women around these averages: 44.8 per cent had between three and six births, and 63.3 per cent had between two and seven births. The number of children borne ranges from none in the case of 211 women to sixteen in the case of three women. If, however, one arbitrarily defines ten or more deliveries as excessive fertility, then 157 or 6.2 per cent of the 2,469 women are of this nature. All of the excessively fertile, except thirteen, are older women—over 35 years of age—who have experienced many years of married life. Yet it is clear that older age or a long period of married life merely provides the opportunity for,

73

rather than necessitates, excessive fertility. Only 144 (12.5 per cent) of the women over 35 years of age are, by the above definition, excessively fertile.

The infertile are primarily young women or those who have experienced just a few years of married life. Over half of them are less than

TABLE 60

Number and Percentage of Women in Different Age Groups Giving Birt Various Numbers of Children

| NUMBER OF CHILDREN EVER BORN | NUMBER | | | | | PERCENTAGE | | | | |
|---|---|---|---|---|---|---|---|---|---|---|
| | Under 25 yrs. | 25–34 yrs. | 35–44 yrs. | Over 45 yrs. | Total | Under 25 yrs. | 25–34 yrs. | 35–44 yrs. | Over 45 yrs. | T |
| 0 | 116 | 49 | 25 | 21 | 211 | 22.7 | 6.1 | 4.0 | 3.9 | |
| 1 | 144 | 56 | 16 | 15 | 231 | 28.2 | 6.9 | 2.6 | 2.8 | |
| 2 | 106 | 105 | 36 | 29 | 276 | 20.7 | 13.0 | 5.8 | 5.4 | 1 |
| 3 | 78 | 142 | 37 | 36 | 293 | 15.3 | 17.5 | 6.0 | 6.7 | 1 |
| 4 | 43 | 138 | 75 | 55 | 311 | 8.4 | 17.1 | 12.2 | 10.2 | 1 |
| 5 | 15 | 114 | 72 | 56 | 257 | 2.9 | 14.1 | 11.7 | 10.4 | 1 |
| 6 | 7 | 97 | 94 | 49 | 247 | 1.4 | 12.0 | 15.4 | 9.1 | 1 |
| 7 | 2 | 49 | 69 | 58 | 178 | 0.4 | 6.1 | 11.3 | 10.8 | |
| 8 | — | 34 | 61 | 84 | 179 | — | 4.2 | 10.0 | 15.6 | |
| 9 | — | 12 | 67 | 50 | 129 | — | 1.4 | 11.0 | 9.3 | |
| 10 | — | 7 | 31 | 34 | 72 | — | 0.9 | 5.1 | 6.3 | |
| 11 | — | 5 | 15 | 25 | 45 | — | 0.6 | 2.5 | 4.7 | |
| 12 | — | 1 | 6 | 11 | 18 | — | 0.1 | 1.0 | 2.1 | |
| 13 | — | — | 2 | 6 | 8 | — | — | 0.3 | 1.1 | |
| 14 | — | — | 4 | 3 | 7 | — | — | 0.7 | 0.6 | |
| 15 | — | — | 1 | 3 | 4 | — | — | 0.2 | 0.6 | |
| 16 | — | — | 1 | 2 | 3 | — | — | 0.2 | 0.4 | |
| Total | 511 | 809 | 612 | 537 | 2469 | 100.0 | 100.0 | 100.0 | 100.0 | 10( |
| (Mean Fertility) | (1.8) | (3.9) | (6.0) | (6.4) | (4.6) | | | | | |

25 years old. The infertile constitute 22.7 per cent of the women in this age group, 6.1 per cent of those 25–34 years old, 4.0 per cent of those 35–44 years old, and 3.9 per cent of those over 45 years of age.

Table 60 also shows the relation of fertility to present age. Women who have completed their reproductive life—those over 45 years of age—have, on the average, 6.4 live births. The average number is 6.0 for those 35–44 years old, 3.9 for those 25–34 years old, and 1.8 for those less than 25 years of age. These averages reflect, of course, the presence of both fertile and infertile women, and the latter, we noted above, are quite numerous in the youngest age group. If the infertile are excluded and averages are then computed, the above averages are found to rise as follows: from 6.4 to 6.7, from 6.0 to 6.2, from 3.9 to 4.2, and from 1.8 to 2.3. The rise in all age groups, except the youngest one, is rather small, and it shows the slight degree to which their averages are affected by the presence of infertile women.

## DURATION OF MARRIAGE AND FERTILITY

It is also evident from our data that the number of children borne by the majority of women is far below the number which they could have had. In the absence of sterility, the number of children which

BLE 61

mber of Women Giving Birth to Various Numbers of Children by Duration Marriage

| MBER OF ILDREN ER BORN | NUMBER OF WOMEN BY DURATION OF MARRIAGE (IN YEARS) | | | | | | | | Total |
|---|---|---|---|---|---|---|---|---|---|
| | 0–2 | 3–7 | 8–12 | 13–17 | 18–22 | 23–27 | 28–32 | Over 33 | |
| 0 | 53 | 60 | 36 | 19 | 13 | 12 | 7 | 11 | 211 |
| 1 | 32 | 96 | 44 | 21 | 14 | 9 | 6 | 9 | 231 |
| 2 | 2 | 83 | 71 | 45 | 26 | 17 | 11 | 21 | 276 |
| 3 | — | 48 | 108 | 50 | 32 | 18 | 7 | 30 | 293 |
| 4 | — | 17 | 64 | 88 | 44 | 32 | 28 | 38 | 311 |
| 5 | — | 2 | 34 | 65 | 57 | 33 | 25 | 41 | 257 |
| 6 | — | — | 22 | 47 | 57 | 40 | 36 | 45 | 247 |
| 7 | — | — | 5 | 21 | 31 | 35 | 34 | 52 | 178 |
| 8 | — | — | 2 | 10 | 30 | 30 | 41 | 66 | 179 |
| 9 | — | — | — | 5 | 15 | 22 | 32 | 55 | 129 |
| 10 | — | — | — | 1 | 8 | 17 | 12 | 34 | 72 |
| 11 | — | — | — | 1 | 3 | 1 | 17 | 23 | 45 |
| 12 | — | — | — | — | 1 | 6 | 3 | 8 | 18 |
| 13 | — | — | — | — | — | 1 | 3 | 4 | 8 |
| 14 | — | — | — | — | — | — | 4 | 3 | 7 |
| 15 | — | — | — | — | — | 2 | — | 2 | 4 |
| 16 | — | — | — | — | — | — | — | 3 | 3 |
| otal | 87 | 306 | 386 | 373 | 331 | 275 | 266 | 445 | 2469 |
| Mean ertility) | (0.4) | (1.6) | (2.9) | (4.1) | (5.1) | (5.9) | (6.7) | (6.8) | (4.6) |

a women could have is roughly equal to her number of years of married life between puberty and menopause. The degree to which actual fertility falls below potential fertility may be crudely measured by our data in Table 61. One observes, for example, that the mean number of births is 2.9 for women who have been married 8–12 years, 4.1 for those who have been married 13–17 years, and 5.1 for those who have been married 18–22 years.

*SPACING OF BIRTHS*

The distribution of births by duration of marriage indicates that there may be a long interval between one birth and the next. The specific ways in which spacing occurs is shown in Table 62. On the

TABLE 62
Intervals Between Births Among Women Having One to Four Deliveries

| LENGTH OF INTERVAL (IN YEARS) | NUMBER OF WOMEN | | | | PERCENTAGE OF WOMEN | | | |
|---|---|---|---|---|---|---|---|---|
| | Marr.–1st Birth | 1st–2nd Birth | 2nd–3rd Birth | 3rd–4th Birth | Marr.–1st Birth | 1st–2nd Birth | 2nd–3rd Birth | 3rd–4th Birth |
| Less than 2.0 | 486 | 535 | 298 | 312 | 21.5 | 26.4 | 17.0 | 21. |
| 2.0– 3.9 | 804 | 614 | 900 | 665 | 35.6 | 30.3 | 51.4 | 45. |
| 4.0– 5.9 | 280 | 509 | 361 | 319 | 12.4 | 25.1 | 20.6 | 21. |
| 6.0– 7.9 | 235 | 142 | 119 | 141 | 10.4 | 7.0 | 6.8 | 9. |
| 8.0– 9.9 | 201 | 134 | 62 | 21 | 8.9 | 6.6 | 3.5 | 1. |
| 10.0–14.9 | 165 | 59 | 11 | — | 7.3 | 2.9 | 0.7 | — |
| 15.0–19.9 | 70 | 34 | — | — | 3.1 | 1.7 | — | — |
| 20 or more | 17 | — | — | — | 0.8 | — | — | — |
| Total | 2258 | 2027 | 1751 | 1458 | 100.0 | 100.0 | 100.0 | 100. |
| (Mean Interval) | (5.1) | (4.1) | (3.7) | (3.5) | | | | |

average, there is an interval of 5.1 years between marriage and first delivery and an interval of 4.1 years between first delivery and second delivery. The intervals between successive births of all kinds average out to 3.8 years.

*MARITAL STATUS AND FERTILITY*

At this point, the distribution of women by marital status and the relation of marital status to fertility can be considered. With respect to marital status, the 2469 women are distributed as follows: 93.7

per cent are married; 2.4 per cent are remarried and 3.9 per cent are widowed. The percentage of widows in our group is certainly much less than the percentage of widows in the general population. Our contact with so few of them is the result of two factors: first, most

BLE 63

nber and Percentage of Women of Different Marital Statuses Giving Birth 'arious Numbers of Children

| BER OF DREN BORN | NUMBER | | | | PERCENTAGE | | | |
|---|---|---|---|---|---|---|---|---|
| | Married | Remarried | Widowed | Total | Married | Remarried | Widowed | Total |
| | 206 | 2 | 3 | 211 | 8.9 | 3.4 | 3.1 | 8.6 |
| | 221 | 6 | 4 | 231 | 9.5 | 10.2 | 4.2 | 9.4 |
| | 262 | 9 | 5 | 276 | 11.3 | 15.2 | 5.2 | 11.2 |
| | 272 | 8 | 13 | 293 | 11.8 | 13.6 | 13.5 | 11.9 |
| | 291 | 10 | 10 | 311 | 12.5 | 16.9 | 10.4 | 12.5 |
| | 242 | 5 | 10 | 257 | 10.5 | 8.5 | 10.4 | 10.4 |
| | 226 | 5 | 16 | 247 | 9.8 | 8.5 | 16.7 | 10.0 |
| | 165 | 2 | 11 | 178 | 7.2 | 3.4 | 11.4 | 7.3 |
| | 165 | 7 | 7 | 179 | 7.1 | 11.8 | 7.3 | 7.3 |
| | 120 | 3 | 6 | 129 | 5.2 | 5.1 | 6.3 | 5.2 |
| | 67 | — | 5 | 72 | 2.9 | — | 5.2 | 2.9 |
| | 42 | 1 | 2 | 45 | 1.8 | 1.7 | 2.1 | 1.8 |
| | 14 | — | 4 | 18 | 0.6 | — | 4.2 | 0.6 |
| | 8 | — | — | 8 | 0.4 | — | — | 0.3 |
| | 7 | — | — | 7 | 0.3 | — | — | 0.3 |
| | 3 | 1 | — | 4 | 0.1 | 1.7 | — | 0.2 |
| | 3 | — | — | 3 | 0.1 | — | — | 0.1 |
| tal | 2314 | 59 | 96 | 2469 | 100.0 | 100.0 | 100.0 | 100.0 |
| lean rtility) | (4.5) | (4.5) | (5.7) | (4.6) | | | | |

widows occupy a secondary position in the household; and, secondly, we selected only heads of households (and their spouses) as interviewees.

According to Table 63, the average number of children ever born is 5.7 for widows and 4.5 for both married women and remarried women. The fertility of widows is impressive and unexpected because of the general belief that they are considerably less fertile than married women. This unexpected finding may, however, be the result of differences between widows and others in present age and, presumably, the number of years of married life. According to Table 64, over half of the widows, 20.2 per cent of the married women, and 32.2 per cent of the remarried women are more than 45 years old. Conversely, none of the widows but 21.8 per cent of the married and 8.5 per cent of the remarried are less than 25 years old. A clear picture of the fertility of these groups may thus be obtained by equating them on the basis of present age. When this is done, as shown in Table 65, married women are found to be slightly more fertile than widows and much more fertile than remarried women of the same age. However, even when age is controlled, widows still exceed remarried women in fertility. One factor which seems to explain this is the low probability of highly fertile women being selected as a marital partner after the death of the first spouse. Since all of the remarried women were once widowed, their fertility during their first marriages may be compared with that of widows in order to measure the effect of high fertility on the chance of remarriage. This comparison, which is presented in Table 66, shows that only one of the 59 remarried women had as many as six deliveries during her first marriage. On the other hand, 51 of the 96 widows—those who never remarried—had this number. In terms of probability, it may, therefore, be said that a woman with six or more deliveries when the first marriage is terminated has one chance in 52 of being remarried. An infertile woman, on the other hand, has a very high probability (20/23) of being remarried. Furthermore, as column 5 shows, this probability of remarriage decreases regularly with increasing fertility.

In addition to the number of children borne by a woman, her age at widowhood also influences the probability of remarriage. We find that remarriage occurred for 89.1 per cent (41/46) of the women who were less than 25 years old when widowed, 32.6 per cent (15/46) of those who were 25–34 years old, and 8.1 per cent (3/37) of those who were 35–44 years old. Remarriage did not occur for any of the twenty-six women who were over 45 years old when widowed. The manner in which fertility and age at widowhood interact to determine the probability of remarriage may be indicated by two general observations. First, within each age category except the oldest one, the percentage of widows who remarried declines as fertility rises. For example, in

TABLE 64

Age Distribution of Women Classified by Marital Status

| AGE IN YEARS) | NUMBER | | | | PERCENTAGE | | | |
|---|---|---|---|---|---|---|---|---|
| | Married | Remarried | Widowed | Total | Married | Remarried | Widowed | Total |
| Under 25 | 506 | 5 | — | 511 | 21.8 | 8.5 | — | 20.7 |
| 25–34 | 778 | 18 | 13 | 809 | 33.6 | 30.5 | 13.5 | 32.8 |
| 35–44 | 564 | 17 | 31 | 612 | 24.4 | 28.8 | 32.3 | 24.8 |
| 45 or more | 466 | 19 | 52 | 537 | 20.2 | 32.2 | 54.2 | 21.7 |
| Total | 2314 | 59 | 96 | 2469 | 100.0 | 100.0 | 100.0 | 100.0 |

TABLE 65

Mean Number of Children Ever Born to Women Classified by Marital Status and Age

| Age (in years) | Married | Remarried | Widowed | Total |
|---|---|---|---|---|
| Under 25 | 1.8 | 1.4 | — | 1.8 |
| 25–34 | 4.0 | 3.1 | 3.7 | 3.9 |
| 35–44 | 6.0 | 5.5 | 5.7 | 6.0 |
| 45 or more | 6.5 | 5.8 | 6.0 | 6.4 |

TABLE 66

Relation of Number of Children Born During First Marriage to the Remarriage of Widows

| NUMBER OF CHILDREN DURING FIRST MARRIAGE | NUMBER OF WIDOWS | | | PERCENTAGE OF TOTAL REMARRIED |
|---|---|---|---|---|
| | Never Remarried | Remarried | Total | |
| 0 | 3 | 20 | 23 | 86.9 |
| 1 | 4 | 14 | 18 | 77.8 |
| 2 | 5 | 9 | 14 | 64.3 |
| 3 | 13 | 8 | 21 | 38.1 |
| 4 | 10 | 5 | 15 | 33.3 |
| 5 | 10 | 2 | 12 | 16.7 |
| 6 or more | 51 | 1 | 52 | 1.9 |
| Total | 96 | 59 | 155 | 38.0 |

the youngest age group, remarriage occurred for 96.6 per cent (28/29) of the widows having less than two births, 78.6 per cent (11/14) of those having two or three births, and 66.7 per cent (2/3) of those having four or five births. Secondly, irrespective of their fertility, women who are widowed after age 45 have no chance of remarriage; and, irrespective of their age at widowhood, women who have six or more births have virtually no chance of remarriage. With regard to the latter group, we find that remarriage occurred for only one of the thirteen who were widowed before age 35 and for none of the thirty-nine who were widowed after age 35. It may, therefore, be concluded from our total data that the probability of remarriage is a function of both a woman's fertility and her age at the time of widowhood.

There is one other observation about marital status and fertility which is especially important. Comparison of column 6 with column 9 of Table 63 shows that there is little difference between the distribution of children among married women and the distribution of children among women of all marital statuses. This is, of course, due to the fact that widowed and remarried women have a small representation in the total group. Since the fertility performance of married women is so close to that of women of all marital statuses, it seems justifiable to base our subsequent analyses on information obtained from married women. The exclusion of widows and remarried women would seem not to distort our findings, and it would allow us to present and discuss them in a clear manner. Our 2314 married women and their spouses, then, are the reference group in the remaining analyses.

*BIRTH CONTROL TECHNIQUES AND FERTILITY*

During the course of the survey, each couple was asked several questions about its knowledge of, use of, and interest in methods of limiting family size. The detailed responses to these questions are presented in Chapter Seven. At this point, attention is given to the effect of birth control techniques on fertility performance.

Of the 2314 couples whom we contacted, only 127 (5.5 per cent) stated that they had ever attempted to limit family size. The method

TABLE 67

Percentage Distribution of Number of Children Ever Born to Couples Classified by Use or Non-Use of Birth Control Techniques (Per cent)

| Number of Children Ever Born | Non-Use of Techniques (2187)* | Some Use of Techniques (127)* | Total (2314)* |
|---|---|---|---|
| None | 9.2 | 3.2 | 8.9 |
| 1–3 | 32.1 | 41.6 | 32.6 |
| 4–6 | 32.6 | 37.1 | 32.8 |
| 7–9 | 19.9 | 11.7 | 19.5 |
| 10 or more | 6.2 | 6.4 | 6.2 |
| Total | 100.0 | 100.0 | 100.0 |
| (Mean Fertility) | (4.5) | (4.5) | (4.5) |

* In this and subsequent tables, the figures in this row refer to the number of couples in each group.

TABLE 68

Mean Number of Children Ever Born to Couples Classified by Use or Non-Use of Birth Control Techniques and Age of Wife

| Age of Wife (in years) | Non-Use of Techniques (2187) | Some Use of Techniques (127) | Total (2314) |
|---|---|---|---|
| Under 25 | 1.8 | 1.8 | 1.8 |
| 25–34 | 4.0 | 3.7 | 4.0 |
| 35–44 | 6.0 | 5.9 | 6.0 |
| 45 or more | 6.4 | 7.0 | 6.5 |
| All ages | | | |
| Arithmetic | 4.5 | 4.5 | 4.5 |
| Weighted* | 4.5 | 4.5 | 4.5 |

* The weighted means in this and subsequent tables are intended to answer the following question: What general fertility averages would different strata have if their age distributions were identical? In computing the weighted means, we have, therefore, acted as if each stratum had the following age distribution: 506 women under 25 years of age; 778 women 25–34 years of age; 564 women 35–44 years of age; and 466 women over 45 years of age (see column 2 of Table 64). The fertility average of each age group is then multiplied by the appropriate constant, and the products thus obtained are cumulated and divided by 2314 (total number of married women or couples) in order to obtain a weighted mean for the stratum.

81

usually chosen was sexual abstinence, but neither it nor other techniques were ordinarily used on a regular basis over a long period of time. It is probably because of the irregular and improper use of techniques that the fertility of users turns out to be identical to that of non-users. According to Table 67, the mean number of children ever born is 4.5 for each group. This identity would, of course, have little meaning if the two groups differed greatly in age structure. But this is not the case, the median age of wives being 33.4 years for non-users and 32.5 years for users. Furthermore, when wives are classified by age groups, non-users and users of the same age are either identical or very similar in fertility.

*FAMILY STRUCTURE AND FERTILITY*

There appears to be a close connection between family structure and fertility. According to Table 69, the mean number of children ever born is 4.4 for couples having a nuclear family and 4.9 for those having a joint-family. However, wives of the latter group tend to be older and this may account for their higher fertility. When the two groups are equated on the basis of the wife's present age, the difference in fertility virtually disappears. As Table 70 shows, the weighted means are 4.4 and 4.5 for couples in the nuclear family and joint-family, respectively. On this basis, it may be concluded that family structure has little bearing on the fertility of couples.

TABLE 69

Percentage Distribution of Number of Children Ever Born to Couples Classified by Family Structure

(Per cent)

| Number of Children Ever Born | Nuclear Family (1619) | Joint Family (695) | Total (2314) |
|---|---|---|---|
| None | 8.7 | 9.6 | 8.9 |
| 1–3 | 33.8 | 30.0 | 32.6 |
| 4–6 | 34.6 | 28.8 | 32.8 |
| 7–9 | 17.9 | 23.0 | 19.5 |
| 10 or more | 5.0 | 8.6 | 6.2 |
| Total | 100.0 | 100.0 | 100.0 |
| (Mean Fertility) | (4.4) | (4.9) | (4.5) |

TABLE 70

Mean Number of Children Ever Born to Couples Classified by Family Structure and Age of Wife

| Age of Wife (in years) | Nuclear Family (1619) | Joint Family (695) | Total (2314) |
|---|---|---|---|
| Under 25 | 1.9 | 1.5 | 1.8 |
| 25–34 | 4.1 | 4.0 | 4.0 |
| 35–44 | 6.0 | 6.0 | 6.0 |
| 45 or more | 5.9 | 6.9 | 6.5 |
| All ages | | | |
| Arithmetic | 4.4 | 4.9 | 4.5 |
| Weighted | 4.4 | 4.5 | 4.5 |

*AGE AT MARRIAGE AND FERTILITY*

Table 71 presents the relationship between the wife's age at marriage and fertility. The mean number of children ever born is 5.3 for those who married before reaching 13 years of age, 4.1 for those who married when 13–17 years of age, and 3.5 for those who married when 18 years of age or older. However, as we noted in Chapter Four, those who marry late (after age 18) tend to be younger women and this may account for their relatively low fertility. It is therefore important to assess the effect of age at marriage on fertility after

TABLE 71

Percentage Distribution of Number of Children Ever Born to Couples Classified by Wife's Age at Marriage
(Per cent)

| Number of Children Ever Born | Under 13 yrs. (897) | 13–17 yrs. (1002) | 18 yrs. or more (415) | Total (2314) |
|---|---|---|---|---|
| None | 6.0 | 10.5 | 11.3 | 8.9 |
| 1–3 | 25.4 | 33.3 | 46.3 | 32.6 |
| 4–6 | 32.7 | 33.9 | 30.4 | 32.8 |
| 7–9 | 27.6 | 16.7 | 8.4 | 19.5 |
| 10 or more | 8.3 | 5.6 | 3.6 | 6.2 |
| Total | 100.0 | 100.0 | 100.0 | 100.0 |
| (Mean Fertility) | (5.3) | (4.1) | (3.5) | (4.5) |

83

equating the couples on the basis of the wife's present age. When this is done, as shown in Table 72, the inverse relationship between age at marriage and fertility still remains. Comparison of the weighted means in this table shows that those who married when 13–17 years of age are 8.0 per cent less fertile and those who married

TABLE 72

Mean Number of Children Ever Born to Couples Classified by Wife's Age at Marriage and Present Age

| Present Age (in years) | Under 13 yrs. (897) | 13–17 yrs. (1002) | 18 yrs. or more (415) | Total (2314) |
|---|---|---|---|---|
| Under 25 | 2.2 | 1.7 | 1.1 | 1.8 |
| 25–34 | 4.7 | 4.1 | 2.9 | 4.0 |
| 35–44 | 6.6 | 5.8 | 4.8 | 6.0 |
| 45 or more | 6.5 | 6.9 | 5.6 | 6.5 |
| All Ages | | | | |
| Arithmetic | 5.3 | 4.1 | 3.5 | 4.5 |
| Weighted | 5.0 | 4.6 | 3.5 | 4.5 |

at 18 years of age or older are 30.0 per cent less fertile than women who married before reaching 13 years of age.

In summary, our analyses show that high fertility is associated with both joint-family living and early age at marriage but is not associated with the use or non-use of birth control techniques. However, the association between high fertility and the joint-family virtually disappears when wives of the nuclear family and those of the joint-family are equated on the basis of present age. This particular analysis therefore reveals, as is generally known, the importance of controlling age differences when comparing the fertility performance of social groups. Such control has little impact on the association between high fertility and early age at marriage.

## SOCIO-ECONOMIC PATTERNS

Our subsequent analyses are concerned with the patterns of fertility among couples who are distinguished on the basis of residence, religion, caste, economic status, or educational achievement. In view of our previous findings, it will be necessary to learn whether differences among the strata in fertility are related to variations in either their present age or age at marriage. The effect of present age on fertility will be ascertained by the method used in our analysis of family structure and fertility, namely: the wives of each stratum are placed in four age groups; fertility averages are computed for the age groups; and these averages are multiplied by certain constants, then cumulated, and divided by 2314 in order to obtain a weighted mean for the stratum. Comparison of the weighted means will indicate the amount of socio-economic variation in fertility which is not attributable to differences in present age.

These weighted means will also be used when measuring the effect of variations in age at marriage on the fertility averages. Our procedure will consist simply of observing whether there is any direct or indirect association between the weighted means and the median ages at marriage for wives of the various strata. Although we have previously shown that low fertility is generally associated with late age at marriage, it does not necessarily follow that a stratum (subgroup) which has a high median age at marriage will be low in fertility. As Table 71 shows, some of the women who marry late (after age 18) are excessively fertile and if they should be concentrated in a particular stratum, this could result in both a high median age at marriage and a high mean fertility.

### RESIDENCE AND FERTILITY

Couples who are distinguished on the basis of residence differ slightly in fertility. According to Table 73, the mean number of children ever born is 4.4 in the city, 4.5 in the towns, and 4.6 in the villages. These differences are quite small and the averages are affected to only a small extent by differences among the wives in present age. As the weighted means in Table 74 show, when age differences are controlled, the fertility averages of the city and village couples remain the same and the average for town couples rises from 4.5 to 4.7. In effect when fertility is related to the ages of wives in the three areas, the town couples are the most fertile and the city couples

TABLE 73
Percentage Distribution of Number of Children Ever Born to Couples
Classified by Residence
(Per cent)

| Number of Children Ever Born | City (882) | Town (309) | Village (1123) | Total (2314) |
|---|---|---|---|---|
| None | 8.6 | 11.0 | 8.6 | 8.9 |
| 1–3 | 34.7 | 31.8 | 31.2 | 32.6 |
| 4–6 | 32.2 | 32.6 | 33.2 | 32.8 |
| 7–9 | 17.8 | 17.5 | 21.3 | 19.5 |
| 10 or more | 6.7 | 7.1 | 5.7 | 6.2 |
| Total | 100.0 | 100.0 | 100.0 | 100.0 |
| (Mean fertility) | (4.4) | (4.5) | (4.6) | (4.5) |

TABLE 74
Mean Number of Children Ever Born to Couples Classified by
Residence and Age of Wife

| Age of Wife (in years) | City (882) | Town (309) | Village (1123) | Total (2314) |
|---|---|---|---|---|
| Under 25 | 1.9 | 1.7 | 1.7 | 1.8 |
| 25–34 | 3.8 | 4.2 | 4.2 | 4.0 |
| 35–44 | 5.7 | 6.2 | 6.3 | 6.0 |
| 45 or more | 6.6 | 7.1 | 6.3 | 6.5 |
| All Ages | | | | |
| Arithmetic | 4.4 | 4.5 | 4.6 | 4.5 |
| Weighted | 4.4 | 4.7 | 4.6 | 4.5 |

FIGURE 1
Median Age at Marriage and Mean Fertility of Wives by Residence

Mean
Fertility

```
4.7  ───────────────────  Town
4.6  ─────────────────  Village
4.5
4.4  ───────────────────────────────────  City
                                                              16.0
         13.0              14.0             15.0
              Median Age at Marriage
```

are the least fertile, but the differences among the areas are still quite small.

There is neither a direct nor an indirect relation between the fertility averages and the median ages at marriage for wives in the three areas. According to Figure 1, the town group is highest in fertility but occupies an intermediate position with respect to age at marriage.

## RELIGION, CASTE, AND FERTILITY

There is considerable variation among religious groups in fertility. According to Table 75, the mean number of children ever born is 4.8

TABLE 75
Percentage Distribution of Number of Children Ever Born to Couple Classified by Religion
(Per cent)

| Number of Children Ever Born | Hindu (1923) | Buddhist (237) | Muslim (97) | Other (57) | Total (2314) |
|---|---|---|---|---|---|
| None | 9.2 | 5.1 | 13.4 | 7.0 | 8 9 |
| 1–3 | 32.9 | 31.7 | 28.9 | 33.3 | 32.6 |
| 4–6 | 32.6 | 34.5 | 27.8 | 40.3 | 32.8 |
| 7–9 | 19.0 | 22.8 | 20.6 | 17.6 | 19.5 |
| 10 or more | 6.3 | 5.9 | 9.3 | 1.8 | 6.2 |
| Total | 100.0 | 100.0 | 100.0 | 100.0 | 100.0 |
| (Mean fertility) | (4.5) | (4.8) | (4.5) | (4.3) | (4.5) |

for Buddhists, 4.5 for both Hindus and Muslims, and 4.3 for "Other Religions" (Jains, Sikhs, Parsees, and Christians). The low average for "Other Religions" does not result from their having a large number of infertile women. Rather, there is a marked tendency among them to give birth to just a few children. This is especially significant in view of the fact that they are, on the average, older than women in the other religions. When differences in present age are controlled, the difference between the fertility of "Other Religions" and that of Buddhists is greater than before. According to Table 76,

TABLE 76

Mean Number of Children Ever Born to Couples Classified by Religion and Age of Wife

| Age of Wife (in years) | Hindu (1923) | Buddhist (237) | Muslim (97) | Other (57) | Total (2314) |
|---|---|---|---|---|---|
| Under 25 | 1.7 | 2.1 | 1.3 | 2.9 | 1.8 |
| 25–34 | 4.0 | 4.5 | 4.4 | 3.8 | 4.0 |
| 35–44 | 6.0 | 6.5 | 6.2 | 4.5 | 6.0 |
| 45 or more | 6.5 | 6.5 | 6.4 | 5.2 | 6.5 |
| All Ages | | | | | |
| Arithmetic | 4.5 | 4.8 | 4.5 | 4.3 | 4.5 |
| Weighted | 4.5 | 4.9 | 4.6 | 4.1 | 4.5 |

the weighted means are 4.1 and 4.9 for the former and latter, respectively, and 4.5 for Hindus and 4.6 for Muslims.

According to Figure 2, the fertility averages are not associated with the median ages at marriage for wives of the religions. Muslims and Hindus, for example, are virtually identical in fertility but differ greatly in their median ages at marriage.

Table 77 presents the fertility patterns present among various caste groups. The mean number of children ever born is 5.8 for the Scheduled Castes (excluding Mahars) and 3.8 for the Malis. The

FIGURE 2

Median Age at Marriage and Mean Fertility of Wives by Religion

Mean Fertility vs. Median Age at Marriage

## TABLE 77
Percentage Distribution of Number of Children Ever Born to Couples Classified by Caste

| NUMBER OF CHILDREN EVER BORN | Brahmin (215) | Maratha (57) | Kunbi (400) | Mali (124) | Bania* (82) | Kosthi (158) | Sonar** (118) | Teli (212) | Dhobi*** (141) | SCHEDULED CASTES | | Gond (50) | Other (168) | TOTAL HINDUS (1923) |
| --- | --- | --- | --- | --- | --- | --- | --- | --- | --- | --- | --- | --- | --- | --- |
| | | | | | | | | | | Mahar (130) | Other (68) | | | |
| None | 6.5 | 1.8 | 9.7 | 14.5 | 7.3 | 9.5 | 8.5 | 11.8 | 8.5 | 9.2 | 5.9 | 2.0 | 11.9 | 9.2 |
| 1–3 | 38.1 | 43.9 | 32.5 | 41.1 | 35.4 | 23.4 | 33.1 | 28.8 | 31.9 | 32.3 | 26.5 | 32.0 | 34.5 | 32.9 |
| 4–6 | 31.6 | 36.8 | 33.5 | 20.2 | 34.1 | 39.2 | 33.8 | 29.7 | 39.0 | 29.2 | 27.9 | 44.0 | 31.0 | 32.6 |
| 7–9 | 17.7 | 10.5 | 20.3 | 18.6 | 13.4 | 19.6 | 16.1 | 25.9 | 16.3 | 21.6 | 20.6 | 16.0 | 17.2 | 19.0 |
| 10 or more | 6.1 | 7.0 | 4.0 | 5.6 | 9.8 | 8.3 | 8.5 | 3.8 | 4.3 | 7.7 | 19.1 | 6.0 | 5.4 | 6.3 |
| Total | 100.0 | 100.0 | 100.0 | 100.0 | 100.0 | 100.0 | 100.0 | 100.0 | 100.0 | 100.0 | 100.0 | 100.0 | 100.0 | 100.0 |
| (Mean fertility) | (4.3) | (4.7) | (4.4) | (3.8) | (4.5) | (4.9) | (4.6) | (4.5) | (4.2) | (4.7) | (5.8) | (4.8) | (4.2) | (4.5) |

\* Includes other trading castes.
\*\* Includes other artisan castes.
\*\*\* Includes other service castes.

89

TABLE 78

Mean Number of Children Ever Born to Couples Classified by Caste and Age of Wife

| AGE OF WIFE (IN YEARS) | Brahmin (215) | Maratha (57) | Kunbi (400) | Mali (124) | Bania* (82) | Kosthi (158) | Sonar** (118) | Teli (212) | Dhobi*** (141) | SCHEDULED CASTES | | Gond (50) | Other (168) | TOTAL HINDUS (1923) |
|---|---|---|---|---|---|---|---|---|---|---|---|---|---|---|
| | | | | | | | | | | Mahar (130) | Other (68) | | | |
| Under 25 | 1.3 | 2.1 | 1.6 | 1.8 | 1.7 | 2.0 | 1.4 | 1.5 | 1.8 | 2.0 | 2.4 | 3.4 | 1.4 | 1.7 |
| 25–34 | 3.0 | 4.0 | 4.3 | 3.2 | 3.5 | 4.6 | 4.0 | 4.3 | 4.6 | 4.1 | 4.7 | 3.7 | 4.2 | 4.0 |
| 35–44 | 5.6 | 4.9 | 6.0 | 6.1 | 6.3 | 6.2 | 5.5 | 5.8 | 5.7 | 6.4 | 8.4 | 5.8 | 5.5 | 6.0 |
| 45 or more | 7.4 | 8.4 | 6.1 | 7.2 | 6.1 | 6.3 | 6.2 | 7.0 | 5.9 | 5.2 | 9.2 | 6.7 | 6.3 | 6.5 |
| All Ages | | | | | | | | | | | | | | |
| Arithmetic | 4.3 | 4.7 | 4.4 | 3.8 | 4.5 | 4.9 | 4.6 | 4.5 | 4.2 | 4.7 | 5.8 | 4.8 | 4.2 | 4.5 |
| Weighted | 4.1 | 4.7 | 4.5 | 4.5 | 4.3 | 4.8 | 4.3 | 4.6, | 4.5 | 4.4 | 6.0 | 4.8 | 4.3 | 4.5 |

* Includes other trading castes.
** Includes other artisan castes.
*** Includes other service castes.

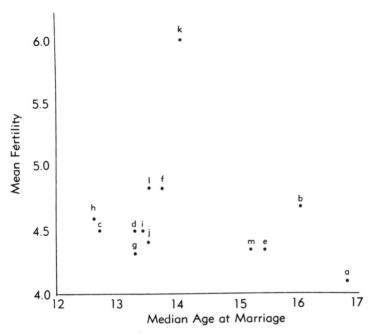

a   Brahmin
b   Maratha
c   Kunbi
d   Mali
e   Bania and other Trading Castes
f   Kosthi
g   Sonar and other Artisan Castes
h   Teli
i   Dhobi, Nai, and other Service Castes
    Scheduled Castes
    j Mahar
    k Other
l   Gond
m   Other

FIGURE 3
Median Age at Marriage and Mean Fertility of Wives by Caste

remaining eleven caste groups have averages ranging from 4.2 live births to 4.9 live births. To a considerable degree, the differences among caste groups in fertility are related to variations among the wives in present age. When age differences are controlled, as shown in Table 78, the low average for Malis rises from 3.8 to 4.5, making this group quite similar in fertility to several other castes. This similarity is also due to the fact that control over age differences produces an increase or decrease in the fertility averages of all caste groups except two. As a result of these changes, the Scheduled Castes, with a weighted mean of 6.0, remain as the most fertile group, but Brahmins, with a weighted mean of 4.1, replace Malis as the least fertile group. The other caste groups whose relative positions are affected by these changes are the Kunbis, Banias, Sonars, Telis, Dhobis, Mahars, and the Gonds.

According to Figure 3, there is neither a direct nor indirect association between the fertility averages and the median ages at marriage for wives in the caste groups.

*OCCUPATION AND FERTILITY*

Table 79 presents the patterns of fertility for couples who are distinguished on the basis of the husband's occupation. The mean number of children ever born is 3.9 for the clerical group and 4.9 for the agricultural group (tenants and owners). In between these extremes are the averages of 4.3 live births for both unskilled workers and traders and 4.5 live births for both artisans and professionals. The differences between some of these groups are due, to a considerable extent, to variations in the present age of their wives. When differences in age are controlled, as shown in Table 80, the average for agriculturalists drops from 4.9 to 4.6 and the average for clerical workers rises from 3.9 to 4.2. Artisans are now found to be as fertile as agriculturalists and more fertile than professionals. The professionals and the unskilled both have weighted means of 4.4 and the traders continue to have a mean of 4.3. In effect, controlling age differences narrows the range in fertility averages for occupational strata and also produces changes in the relative positions of some strata.

92

TABLE 79

Percentage Distribution of Number of Children Ever Born to Couples Classified by Occupation of Husband*

(Per cent)

| Number of Children Ever Born | Unskilled (272) | Artisan (629) | Trade (326) | Clerical (198) | Profess. and Admin. (249) | Agric. (611) | Total (2285) |
|---|---|---|---|---|---|---|---|
| None | 10.7 | 7.0 | 11.3 | 11.1 | 7.2 | 8.2 | 8.9 |
| 1–3 | 35.3 | 33.5 | 33.7 | 36.9 | 35.3 | 27.8 | 32.6 |
| 4–6 | 31.6 | 35.0 | 31.9 | 32.3 | 32.1 | 32.4 | 32.8 |
| 7–9 | 18.4 | 18.0 | 16.3 | 17.2 | 16.5 | 25.0 | 19.5 |
| 10 or more | 4.0 | 6.5 | 6.8 | 2.5 | 8.9 | 6.6 | 6.2 |
| Total | 100.0 | 100.0 | 100.0 | 100.0 | 100.0 | 100.0 | 100.0 |
| (Mean fertility) | (4.3) | (4.5) | (4.3) | (3.9) | (4.5) | (4.9) | (4.5) |

* Excludes 29 couples where the husband was unemployed.

According to Figure 4, there is no association between the fertility averages and the median ages at marriage for wives in the various occupational groups. For example, those in the unskilled group and those in the professional group are identical in fertility but differ greatly in median age at marriage.

TABLE 80

Mean Number of Children Ever Born to Couples Classified by Occupation of Husband* and Age of Wife

| Age of Wife (in years) | Unskilled (272) | Artisan (629) | Trade (326) | Clerical (198) | Profess. and Admin. (249) | Agric. (611) | Total (2285) |
|---|---|---|---|---|---|---|---|
| Under 25 | 1.8 | 1.9 | 1.7 | 1.6 | 1.6 | 1.7 | 1.8 |
| 25–34 | 3.9 | 4.4 | 3.8 | 3.3 | 3.6 | 4.3 | 4.0 |
| 35–44 | 5.6 | 5.9 | 5.9 | 6.0 | 6.0 | 6.2 | 6.0 |
| 45 or more | 6.6 | 6.4 | 6.2 | 6.3 | 6.8 | 6.5 | 6.5 |
| All Ages | | | | | | | |
| Arithmetic | 4.3 | 4.5 | 4.3 | 3.9 | 4.5 | 4.9 | 4.5 |
| Weighted | 4.4 | 4.6 | 4.3 | 4.2 | 4.4 | 4.6 | 4.5 |

* Excludes 29 couples where the husband was unemployed.

93

FIGURE 4

Median Age at Marriage and Mean Fertility of Wives Classified by Husband's Occupation

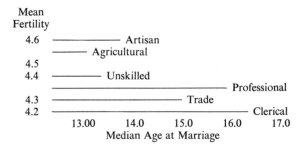

When couples are classified on the basis of the wife's employment status, considerable variation in fertility is evident. According to Table 81, the mean number of children ever born is 4.5 for unemployed wives and 5.0 for employed wives (those working for wages). As Table 82 shows, the difference between their averages remains about the same when they are equated on the basis of present age. Since only two groups are involved in this particular discussion, it would not be meaningful to relate their fertility averages to their median ages at marriage.

TABLE 81

Percentage Distribution of Number of Children Ever Born to Couples Classified by Employment Status of Wife
(Per cent)

| Number of Children Ever Born | Unemployed (2035) | Employed (279) | Total (2314) |
|---|---|---|---|
| None | 9.1 | 7.8 | 8.9 |
| 1–3 | 34.2 | 21.2 | 32.6 |
| 4–6 | 31.9 | 39.1 | 32.8 |
| 7–9 | 18.7 | 25.1 | 19.5 |
| 10 or more | 6.1 | 6.8 | 6.2 |
| Total | 100.0 | 100.0 | 100.0 |
| (Mean fertility) | (4.5) | (5.0) | (4.5) |

TABLE 82

Mean Number of Children Ever Born to Couples Classified by Employment Status and Age of Wife

| Age of Wife (in years) | Unemployed (2035) | Employed (279) | Total (2314) |
|---|---|---|---|
| Under 25 | 1.7 | 1.9 | 1.8 |
| 25–34 | 3.9 | 4.6 | 4.0 |
| 35–44 | 6.0 | 5.9 | 6.0 |
| 45 or more | 6.4 | 7.0 | 6.5 |
| All Ages | | | |
| Arithmetic | 4.5 | 5.0 | 4.5 |
| Weighted | 4.4 | 4.8 | 4.5 |

*INCOME, LAND OWNERSHIP, AND FERTILITY*

Couples who are differentiated on the basis of the husband's annual income likewise differ in fertility. According to Table 83, the mean number of children ever born ranges from 3.8 for those earning 1500–1999 rupees to 4.8 for those earning 1000–1499 rupees. The lowest income group, Under 500 rupees, and the highest income group, Over 2000 rupees, have identical averages of 4.6 live births

TABLE 83

Percentage Distribution of Number of Children Ever Born to Couples Classified by Annual Income of Husband

(Per cent)

| Number of Children Ever Born | Under 500 Rs. (650) | 500– 999 Rs. (877) | 1000– 1499 Rs. (360) | 1500– 1999 Rs. (124) | 2000 Rs. or more (303) | Total (2314) |
|---|---|---|---|---|---|---|
| None | 10.6 | 8.8 | 8.1 | 8.1 | 6.9 | 8.9 |
| 1–3 | 29.2 | 33.2 | 31.4 | 40.3 | 36.3 | 32.6 |
| 4–6 | 32.5 | 34.3 | 31.7 | 36.3 | 29.4 | 32.8 |
| 7–9 | 20.8 | 17.8 | 22.4 | 12.1 | 20.8 | 19.5 |
| 10 or more | 6.9 | 5.9 | 6.4 | 3.2 | 6.6 | 6.2 |
| Total | 100.0 | 100.0 | 100.0 | 100.0 | 100.0 | 100.0 |
| (Mean fertility) | (4.6) | (4.4) | (4.8) | (3.8) | (4.6) | (4.5) |

95

which indicates the absence of any direct or indirect association between fertility and income. However, the averages for income categories are, to a considerable extent, affected by variations in the present age of their wives. When age is controlled, as shown in Table 84, the average for those earning 1500–1999 rupees rises from 3.8 to 4.2 and the average for those earning 1000–1499 rupees drops from

TABLE 84
Mean Number of Children Ever Born to Couples Classified by Annual Income of Husband and Age of Wife

| Age of Wife (in years) | Under 500 Rs. (650) | 500– 999 Rs. (877) | 1000– 1499 Rs. (360) | 1500– 1999 Rs. (124) | 2000 Rs. or more (303) | Total (2314) |
|---|---|---|---|---|---|---|
| Under 25 | 1.7 | 1.7 | 2.0 | 1.6 | 1.5 | 1.8 |
| 25–34 | 4.2 | 4.2 | 3.8 | 3.4 | 3.7 | 4.0 |
| 35–44 | 6.2 | 6.0 | 5.9 | 5.4 | 5.8 | 6.0 |
| 45 or more | 6.6 | 6.0 | 7.3 | 6.8 | 6.4 | 6.5 |
| All Ages | | | | | | |
| Arithmetic | 4.6 | 4.4 | 4.8 | 3.8 | 4.6 | 4.5 |
| Weighted | 4.6 | 4.5 | 4.6 | 4.2 | 4.3 | 4.5 |

4.8 to 4.6. The latter group is now identical in fertility to those earning less than 500 rupees. The averages for those earning 500–999 rupees and those earning more than 2000 rupees are now 4.5 and 4.3, respectively. Control over age differences, therefore, narrows the range in fertility averages and also produces a change in the relative positions of some income groups.

According to Figure 5, there is neither a positive nor a negative association between the fertility averages and the median ages at marriage for wives in the various income groups. For example, those in the lowest income group and those in the middle income group are identical in fertility, but differ greatly in age at marriage.

Among land ownership groups, the number of children ever born ranges from 5.0 for the large land owners (20 acres or more) to 4.4 for both the landless and small owners (1–9 acres). The medium owners (10–19 acres) have, on the average, 4.8 live births. If the landless are excluded, then fertility is found to increase with increasing land

FIGURE 5

Median Age at Marriage and Mean Fertility of Wives Classified by Husband's Income

ownership. When differences in the present age of wives in these groups are controlled, as shown in Table 86, the average of the landless rises slightly and the averages for the other three groups drop slightly. The large owners remain as the most fertile and the small owners are now the least fertile whereas previously the latter's average was the same as that of the landless.

According to Figure 6, there is neither a direct nor an indirect relation between the fertility averages and the ages at marriage for wives in the several groups. For example, those in the small ownership group and those in the medium ownership group are almost identical in age at marriage but differ greatly in fertility.

TABLE 85

Percentage Distribution of Number of Children Ever Born to Couples Classified by Land Ownership

(Per cent)

| Number of Children Ever Born | Landless (1308) | 1–9 acres (403) | 10–19 acres (297) | 20 acres or more (306) | Total (2314) |
|---|---|---|---|---|---|
| None | 9.3 | 9.9 | 7.7 | 7.2 | 8.9 |
| 1–3 | 34.6 | 32.0 | 29.0 | 28.6 | 32.6 |
| 4–6 | 32.1 | 34.5 | 33.0 | 33.6 | 32.8 |
| 7–9 | 17.9 | 18.6 | 23.2 | 23.7 | 19.5 |
| 10 or more | 6.1 | 5.0 | 7.1 | 6.9 | 6.2 |
| Total | 100.0 | 100.0 | 100.0 | 100.0 | 100.0 |
| (Mean fertility) | (4.4) | (4.4) | (4.8) | (5.0) | (4.5) |

97

TABLE 86

Mean Number of Children Ever Born to Couples Classified by Land Ownership and Age of Wife

| Age of Wife (in years) | Landless (1308) | 1–9 acres (403) | 10–19 acres (297) | 20 acres or more (306) | Total (2314) |
|---|---|---|---|---|---|
| Under 25 | 1.8 | 1.7 | 1.8 | 1.6 | 1.8 |
| 25–34 | 3.9 | 4.2 | 4.0 | 4.3 | 4.0 |
| 35–44 | 6.0 | 5.5 | 6.2 | 6.4 | 6.0 |
| 45 or more | 6.5 | 6.0 | 6.5 | 7.0 | 6.5 |
| All Ages | | | | | |
| Arithmetic | 4.4 | 4.4 | 4.8 | 5.0 | 4.5 |
| Weighted | 4.5 | 4.3 | 4.6 | 4.8 | 4.5 |

FIGURE 6

Median Age at Marriage and Mean Fertility of Wives Classified by Land Ownership of Husband

*EDUCATION AND FERTILITY*

When couples are classified on the basis of the husband's educational achievement, considerable variation in fertility is again evident. According to Table 87, the mean number of children ever born is 5.0 for the uneducated and 3.9 for both the high school and the college groups. In between these extremes, are the averages of 4.3 livebirths for both the primary school group and matriculates, and 4.1 livebirths for the middle school group. When differences in the present age of wives are controlled, as shown in Table 88, the uneducated remain as the most fertile group although their average drops from 5.0 livebirths to 4.7 livebirths, and the high school group, with an average of 3.9

98

TABLE 87

Percentage Distribution of Number of Children Ever Born to Couples Classified
Education of Husband
(per cent)

| Number of Children Ever Born | No Educ. (891) | Primary School (736) | Middle School (302) | High School (86) | Matri- culation (168) | College (131) | Total (2314) |
|---|---|---|---|---|---|---|---|
| one | 7.9 | 9.9 | 8.9 | 14.0 | 7.7 | 8.4 | 8.9 |
| 3 | 26.3 | 35.9 | 35.1 | 30.2 | 37.5 | 47.3 | 32.6 |
| 6 | 33.0 | 32.2 | 36.1 | 34.9 | 32.1 | 26.0 | 32.8 |
| 9 | 25.7 | 15.6 | 15.6 | 18.6 | 14.9 | 13.7 | 19.5 |
| or more | 7.1 | 6.4 | 4.3 | 2.3 | 7.8 | 4.6 | 6.2 |
| Total | 100.0 | 100.0 | 100.0 | 100.0 | 100.0 | 100.0 | 100.0 |
| (Mean fertility) | (5.0) | (4.3) | (4.1) | (3.9) | (4.3) | (3.9) | (4.5) |

livebirths, remains as the least fertile. The average number of livebirths rises from 3.9 to 4.0 for the college group, from 4.1 to 4.3 for
the middle school group, and from 4.3 to 4.5 for the primary school
group.

According to Figure 7, the fertility averages are not associated
directly or indirectly with the median ages at marriage for wives in the
various educational groups. For example, those in the middle school

TABLE 88

Mean Number of Children Ever Born to Couples Classified by Education
Husband and Age of Wife

| Age of Wife (in years) | No Educ. (891) | Primary School (736) | Middle School (302) | High School (86) | Matri- culation (168) | College (131) | Total (2314) |
|---|---|---|---|---|---|---|---|
| under 25 | 1.6 | 1.9 | 1.7 | 1.7 | 1.6 | 1.5 | 1.8 |
| -34 | 4.4 | 4.0 | 4.1 | 4.2 | 3.4 | 3.0 | 4.0 |
| -44 | 6.3 | 6.1 | 6.0 | 3.8 | 5.9 | 5.1 | 6.0 |
| or more | 6.6 | 6.4 | 5.5 | 6.1 | 7.0 | 7.1 | 6.5 |
| all ages | | | | | | | |
| Arithmetic | 5.0 | 4.3 | 4.1 | 3.9 | 4.3 | 3.9 | 4.5 |
| Weighted | 4.7 | 4.5 | 4.3 | 3.9 | 4.3 | 4.0 | 4.5 |

99

group and those in the matriculate group are identical in fertility but differ greatly in median age at marriage.

When couples are classified on the basis of the wife's educational achievement, fertility is found to be inversely associated with higher

FIGURE 7

Median Age at Marriage and Mean Fertility of Wives Classified by Husband's Education

Mean
Fertility

| | |
|---|---|
| 4.7 | —————— None |
| 4.6 | |
| 4.5 | ————————— Primary |
| 4.4 | |
| 4.3 | ————————————— Middle |
| | ——————————————— Matriculation |
| 4.2 | |
| 4.1 | |
| 4.0 | ———————————————————— College |
| 3.9 | ————————————— High |

13.0   14.0   15.0   16.0   17.0   18.0

Median Age at Marriage

education. According to Table 89, the mean number of children ever born is 4.7 for the uneducated group, 4.3 for the primary school group, and 3.4 for those with more than primary school education. Educated women are, however, younger than the uneducated women, and this may account for the differences in the averages. When differences in present age are controlled, as shown in Table 90, the mean number of livebirths drops from 4.7 to 4.6 for the uneducated group and rises from 4.3 to 4.7 for the primary school group, making them the most fertile of the three groups. Those with more than primary school education remain as the least fertile group.

Their fertility averages are not directly or indirectly associated with their median ages at marriage. For example, the uneducated and those with primary schooling are virtually identical in fertility (4.6 livebirths vs. 4.7 livebirths) but differ greatly in age at marriage (13.4 years vs. 15.7 years).

100

TABLE 89

Percentage Distribution of Number of Children Ever Born to Couples Classified by Education of Wife

(Per cent)

| Ever Born | No Education (1772) | Primary School (318) | Above Primary School (224) | Total (2314) |
|---|---|---|---|---|
| None | 8.9 | 9.8 | 8.0 | 8.9 |
| 1–3 | 30.0 | 35.2 | 50.0 | 32.6 |
| 4–6 | 32.8 | 34.9 | 29.9 | 32.8 |
| 7–9 | 21.3 | 14.8 | 10.7 | 19.5 |
| 10 or more | 7.0 | 5.3 | 1.4 | 6.2 |
| Total | 100.0 | 100.0 | 100.0 | 100.0 |
| (Mean fertility) | (4.7) | (4.3) | (3.4) | (4.5) |

## SUMMARY

The level of fertility in Central India is rather low despite the general absence of deliberate efforts to limit conceptions and births. The mean number of children ever born is 4.6 for women of all ages and 6.4 for women who have completed their reproductive life. Women belonging to joint-families are more fertile than women belonging to nuclear families, but this difference is due solely to the older age of

TABLE 90

Mean Number of Children Ever Born to Couples Classified by Education and Age of Wife

| Age of Wife (in years) | No Education (1772) | Primary School (318) | Above Primary School (224) | Total (2314) |
|---|---|---|---|---|
| Under 25 | 1.8 | 1.7 | 1.6 | 1.8 |
| 25–34 | 4.2 | 4.0 | 3.2 | 4.0 |
| 35–44 | 6.1 | 6.4 | 4.8 | 6.0 |
| 45 or more | 6.5 | 6.8 | 6.2 | 6.5 |
| All Ages | | | | |
| Arithmetic | 4.7 | 4.3 | 3.4 | 4.5 |
| Weighted | 4.6 | 4.7 | 3.8 | 4.5 |

the former group. There is a positive association between fertility and early age at marriage.

There are large variations among the several socio-economic strata in fertility but in several cases the variations are primarily attributable to differences in age distributions. When women are equated on the basis of present age, the fertility differences among residential groups, occupational classes, and among income groups virtually disappear. In the case of the remaining strata, control over age reduces only slightly the fertility differences among them.

# Fertility, Child Mortality, and Socio-Economic Status

OUR data on couple fertility suggest a large growth in the total population of Central India as well as changes in the relative sizes of the various social strata inhabitating this area. But the degree to which these changes are, in fact, occurring depends not only on fertility but also on child mortality. It is, therefore, the purpose of this chapter to indicate the prevalence of child mortality, in general and among various social strata. By comparing these strata in terms of both fertility and child mortality, one may gain a picture of their actual growth patterns. For our purpose, child mortality includes the death of any offspring, irrespective of his or her age at the time of death, which occurred prior to our interview with a couple. This loose definition is necessitated by the fact that we failed to obtain from couples information on the specific ages at which their children died. It is, therefore, possible that some of our cases of child mortality are really offspring who lived to adulthood, married, and produced children. But, on the basis of other studies of mortality, it may be reasonably assumed that the number of such cases is quite small.

## GENERAL PATTERNS

The 2314 couples in our study gave birth to a total of 10,441 offspring. At the time of our survey, 6537 (62.6 per cent) of them were still living and 3904 (37.4 per cent) had died. Child mortality was most frequent among the highly fertile and older couples. As Table 91 shows, the percentage of children claimed by death rises regularly from 22.6 per cent among couples having one child to 39.6 per cent among couples having seven children. The percentages for couples having eight, nine, and ten or more children are 38.6, 44.9, and 41.8, respectively. Child mortality thus reduces considerably the number of children to whom couples must give care and support. For

103

example, as column 7 shows, couples having eight or nine births are left with an average of five living children. For our entire series of cases, the average numbers of births and living children are 4.5 and 2.8 respectively.

TABLE 91
Relation Between Fertility and Child Mortality

| Number of Children Ever Born | Number of Couples | Total Children Ever Born | Total Children Ever Born | | | |
|---|---|---|---|---|---|---|
| | | | | PERCENTAGE | | MEAN NUMBER |
| | | | Living | Dead | Total | LIVING |
| 0 | 206 | — | — | — | — | — |
| 1 | 221 | 221 | 77.4 | 22.6 | 100.0 | 0.8 |
| 2 | 262 | 524 | 71.2 | 28.8 | 100.0 | 1.4 |
| 3 | 272 | 816 | 69.5 | 30.5 | 100.0 | 2.1 |
| 4 | 291 | 1164 | 67.9 | 32.1 | 100.0 | 2.7 |
| 5 | 242 | 1210 | 64.8 | 35.2 | 100.0 | 3.2 |
| 6 | 226 | 1356 | 61.5 | 38.5 | 100.0 | 3.7 |
| 7 | 165 | 1155 | 60.4 | 39.6 | 100.0 | 4.2 |
| 8 | 165 | 1320 | 61.2 | 38.8 | 100.0 | 4.9 |
| 9 | 120 | 1080 | 55.1 | 44.9 | 100.0 | 5.0 |
| 10 or more | 144 | 1595 | 58.2 | 41.8 | 100.0 | 6.4 |
| Total | 2314 | 10441 | 62.6 | 37.4 | 100.0 | 2.8 |

Specific rather than general relationships between fertility and the number of living children are presented in Table 92. Two observations are especially pertinent. First, according to figures in italics, there are 617 couples, having from one to thirteen offspring, who have not experienced a single instance of child mortality. Conversely, there are 108 couples, having from one to nine offspring, who have lost all of their children. Secondly, couples of the same fertility differ considerably in their number of living children. Couples having four offspring may be used to illustrate this point. Of the 291 couples in this fertility group, 79 have four living children, 92 have three living children, 79 have two living children, 31 have one living child, and 10 have lost all of their children.

Table 93 presents the prevalence of child mortality among couples classified by the present age of the wife. As column 6 shows, child mortality rises slightly but regularly as age increases. A positive

**TABLE 92**
Distribution of Couples by Number of Children Ever Born and Number of Living Children

| NUMBER OF CHILDREN EVER BORN | NUMBER OF LIVING CHILDREN | | | | | | | | | | | | | | | TOTAL COUPLES | |
|---|---|---|---|---|---|---|---|---|---|---|---|---|---|---|---|---|---|
| | 0 | 1 | 2 | 3 | 4 | 5 | 6 | 7 | 8 | 9 | 10 | 11 | 12 | 13 | 14 | Number | Per Cent |
| 0 | *206* | — | — | — | — | — | — | — | — | — | — | — | — | — | — | 206 | 8.9 |
| 1 | 50 | *171* | — | — | — | — | — | — | — | — | — | — | — | — | — | 221 | 9.5 |
| 2 | 24 | 104 | *134* | — | — | — | — | — | — | — | — | — | — | — | — | 262 | 11.3 |
| 3 | 11 | 63 | 90 | *108* | — | — | — | — | — | — | — | — | — | — | — | 272 | 11.8 |
| 4 | 10 | 31 | 79 | 92 | *79* | — | — | — | — | — | — | — | — | — | — | 291 | 12.5 |
| 5 | 3 | 27 | 38 | 58 | 72 | *44* | — | — | — | — | — | — | — | — | — | 242 | 10.5 |
| 6 | 5 | 21 | 30 | 54 | 31 | 43 | *42* | — | — | — | — | — | — | — | — | 226 | 9.8 |
| 7 | 3 | 6 | 13 | 27 | 41 | 39 | 26 | *10* | — | — | — | — | — | — | — | 165 | 7.2 |
| 8 | 1 | 2 | 14 | 24 | 27 | 37 | 28 | 15 | *17* | — | — | — | — | — | — | 165 | 7.1 |
| 9 | 1 | 2 | 12 | 17 | 13 | 28 | 21 | 16 | 7 | *3* | — | — | — | — | — | 120 | 5.2 |
| 10 | — | 1 | 3 | 3 | 10 | 9 | 14 | 11 | 9 | 4 | 3 | — | — | — | — | 67 | 2.9 |
| 11 | — | 1 | 1 | 3 | 6 | 6 | 7 | 4 | 4 | 6 | 2 | 2 | — | — | — | 42 | 1.8 |
| 12 | — | — | — | — | 1 | 2 | 2 | 1 | — | 4 | — | 1 | *3* | — | — | 14 | 0.6 |
| 13 | — | — | — | — | 1 | 1 | 2 | 1 | — | 1 | 1 | — | — | *1* | — | 8 | 0.4 |
| 14 | — | — | — | — | 1 | 1 | 2 | 1 | — | 1 | 1 | — | — | — | — | 7 | 0.3 |
| 15 | — | — | — | 1 | — | — | 2 | — | — | — | — | — | — | — | — | 3 | 0.1 |
| 16 | — | — | — | — | — | — | 2 | — | — | — | — | — | — | — | 1 | 3 | 0.1 |
| Number | 314 | 429 | 414 | 387 | 282 | 210 | 148 | 59 | 37 | 19 | 7 | 3 | 3 | 1 | 1 | 2314 | 100.0 |
| Per Cent | 13.6 | 18.5 | 17.9 | 16.7 | 12.3 | 9.1 | 6.4 | 2.5 | 1.6 | 0.8 | 0.3 | 0.1 | 0.1 | 0.1 | | 100.0 | |

association between child mortality and the age of couples is, however, quite normal since many of the children of older couples were born several years before the survey and, consequently, had many years of exposure to the risks of death.

TABLE 93

Fertility and Child Mortality Among Couples Classified by Present Age of Wife

| AGE OF WIFE (IN YEARS) | NUMBER OF COUPLES | MEAN NUMBER OF CHILDREN | | | CHILD MORTALITY (PER CENT) |
|---|---|---|---|---|---|
| | | Living | Deceased | Ever Born | |
| Under 25 | 506 | 1.2 | 0.6 | 1.8 | 33.3 |
| 25–34 | 778 | 2.5 | 1.4 | 3.9 | 35.9 |
| 35–44 | 564 | 3.7 | 2.3 | 6.0 | 38.3 |
| 45 or more | 466 | 3.8 | 2.7 | 6.5 | 41.6 |
| Total | 2314 | 2.8 | 1.7 | 4.5 | 37.4 |

## SOCIO-ECONOMIC PATTERNS

At this point, our various socio-economic strata can be compared with respect to fertility and child mortality. Since child mortality and fertility are associated with the age of couples, it will be necessary to equate socio-economic strata on the basis of age before making any comparisons. Our procedure for equating them is identical to that employed in the previous chapter.

### RESIDENCE AND CHILD MORTALITY

Couples who are distinguished on the basis of residence differ considerably in their prevalence of child mortality. According to Table 94, the percentage of children claimed by death is 44.7 in the towns, 41.3 in the villages, and 33.3 in the city. Because of its relatively low child mortality, the city group, although the least fertile, has the largest average number of living children. Conversely, the town group is the most fertile but has the smallest average number of living children.

## TABLE 94

Fertility and Child Mortality Among Couples Classified by Residence

| RESIDENCE | NUMBER OF COUPLES | MEAN* NUMBER OF CHILDREN | | | CHILD MORTALITY (PER CENT) |
|---|---|---|---|---|---|
| | | Living | Deceased | Ever Born | |
| City | 882 | 3.0 | 1.5 | 4.5 | 33.3 |
| Town | 309 | 2.6 | 2.1 | 4.7 | 44.7 |
| Village | 1123 | 2.7 | 1.9 | 4.6 | 41.3 |
| Total | 2314 | 2.8 | 1.7 | 4.5 | 37.4 |

* The means used in this table and subsequent tables are weighted means. Our procedure in computing them is described in the footnote to Table 68.

### RELIGION, CASTE, AND CHILD MORTALITY

There is considerable variation among religious groups in the prevalence of child mortality. According to Table 95, the percentage of children claimed by death is 40.8 among Buddhists, 37.8 among Hindus, 34.8 among Muslims, and only 17.1 among "Other Religions" (Christians, Sikhs, Parsees, and Jains). Because of their relatively low child mortality, "Other Religions," although the least fertile group, have the largest average number of living children. The average number of living children for Buddhists, the most fertile group, is almost identical to that for Hindus and Muslims.

Table 96 presents the prevalence of child mortality among caste groups. At one extreme are the Brahmins who lost only 17.1 per cent of their children and at the other extreme are the Malis and Scheduled

## TABLE 95

Fertility and Child Mortality Among Couples Classified by Religion

| RELIGION | NUMBER OF COUPLES | MEAN NUMBER OF CHILDREN | | | CHILD MORTALITY (PER CENT) |
|---|---|---|---|---|---|
| | | Living | Deceased | Ever Born | |
| Hindu | 1923 | 2.8 | 1.7 | 4.5 | 37.8 |
| Buddhist | 237 | 2.9 | 2.0 | 4.9 | 40.8 |
| Muslim | 97 | 3.0 | 1.6 | 4.6 | 34.8 |
| Other | 57 | 3.4 | 0.7 | 4.1 | 17.1 |
| Total | 2314 | 2.8 | 1.7 | 4.5 | 37.4 |

Castes (excluding Mahars) who lost over half of their children. Because of low child mortality, the Brahmins, although the least fertile of all castes, have the largest average number of living children. The Scheduled Castes, on the other hand, greatly exceed all others in

TABLE 96

Fertility and Child Mortality Among Couples Classified by Caste

| CASTE | NUMBER OF COUPLES | MEAN NUMBER OF CHILDREN | | | CHILD MORTALITY (PER CENT |
|---|---|---|---|---|---|
| | | Living | Deceased | Ever Born | |
| Brahmin | 215 | 3.4 | 0.7 | 4.1 | 17.1 |
| Maratha | 57 | 2.9 | 1.8 | 4.7 | 38.3 |
| Kunbi | 400 | 2.6 | 1.9 | 4.5 | 42.2 |
| Mali | 124 | 2.2 | 2.3 | 4.5 | 51.1 |
| Bania and other trading castes | 82 | 3.2 | 1.1 | 4.3 | 25.6 |
| Kosthi | 158 | 2.8 | 2.0 | 4.8 | 41.7 |
| Sonar, lohar and other artisan castes | 118 | 2.7 | 1.6 | 4.3 | 37.2 |
| Teli | 212 | 2.8 | 1.8 | 4.6 | 39.1 |
| Dhobi, nai and other service castes | 141 | 2.4 | 2.1 | 4.5 | 46.7 |
| Scheduled castes | | | | | |
| Mahar | 130 | 2.6 | 1.8 | 4.4 | 40.9 |
| Other | 68 | 2.9 | 3.1 | 6.0 | 51.7 |
| Gond | 50 | 2.8 | 2.0 | 4.8 | 41.7 |
| Other | 168 | 2.8 | 1.5 | 4.3 | 34.9 |
| Total Hindus | 1923 | 2.8 | 1.7 | 4.5 | 37.8 |

fertility but their average number of living children does not differ significantly from that of Marathas, Kosthis, Telis, Gonds, and Other Castes.

*OCCUPATION AND CHILD MORTALITY*

Table 97 presents the frequency of child mortality among couples distinguished by the husband's occupation. The percentage of children claimed by death is 27.3 among professionals, 30.4 among agriculturalists, 41.3 among artisans, and about 34 among unskilled workers, traders, and clerical workers. Child mortality reduces the average number of children among agriculturalists and artisans from 4.6 to 3.2 and from 4.6 to 2.7, respectively. The reduction for clerical

108

TABLE 97

Fertility and Child Mortality Among Couples Classified by Occupation of Husband*

| OCCUPATIONAL GROUP | NUMBER OF COUPLES | MEAN NUMBER OF CHILDREN | | | CHILD MORTALITY (PER CENT) |
| --- | --- | --- | --- | --- | --- |
| | | Living | Deceased | Ever Born | |
| Unskilled | 272 | 2.9 | 1.5 | 4.4 | 34.1 |
| Artisan | 629 | 2.7 | 1.9 | 4.6 | 41.3 |
| Trade | 326 | 2.8 | 1.5 | 4.3 | 34.9 |
| Clerical | 198 | 2.8 | 1.4 | 4.2 | 33.3 |
| Professional and Admin. | 249 | 3.2 | 1.2 | 4.4 | 27.3 |
| Agricultural | 611 | 3.2 | 1.4 | 4.6 | 30.4 |
| Total | 2285 | 2.8 | 1.7 | 4.5 | 37.4 |

* Excludes 29 couples where the husband was unemployed.

workers is from 4.2 children to 2.8 children. Thus, because of their high child mortality, artisans, who are one of the most fertile groups, have fewer living children, on the average, than clerical workers, who are the least fertile group.

Among couples distinguished by the employment status of the wife rather than the husband, there is little difference in child mortality. The percentage of children claimed by death is 36.4 for the unemployed and 37.5 for the employed. Consequently, the unemployed and the employed differ in their average number of living children (2.8 vs. 3.0) to about the same extent as they differ in average fertility (4.4 vs. 4.8).

TABLE 98

Fertility and Child Mortality Among Couples by Employment Status of Wife

| EMPLOYMENT STATUS OF WIFE | NUMBER OF COUPLES | MEAN NUMBER OF CHILDREN | | | CHILD MORTALITY (PER CENT) |
| --- | --- | --- | --- | --- | --- |
| | | Living | Deceased | Ever Born | |
| Unemployed | 2035 | 2.8 | 1.6 | 4.4 | 36.4 |
| Employed | 279 | 3.0 | 1.8 | 4.8 | 37.5 |
| Total | 2314 | 2.8 | 1.7 | 4.5 | 37.4 |

TABLE 99

Fertility and Child Mortality Among Couples Classified by Annual Income of Husband

| ANNUAL INCOME (IN RUPEES) | NUMBER OF COUPLES | MEAN NUMBER OF CHILDREN | | | CHILD MORTALITY (PER CENT) |
|---|---|---|---|---|---|
| | | Living | Deceased | Ever Born | |
| Under 500 | 650 | 2.6 | 2.0 | 4.6 | 43.5 |
| 500–999 | 877 | 2.7 | 1.8 | 4.5 | 40.0 |
| 1000–1499 | 360 | 3.1 | 1.5 | 4.6 | 32.6 |
| 1500–1999 | 124 | 2.7 | 1.5 | 4.2 | 35.7 |
| 2000 or more | 303 | 3.4 | 0.9 | 4.3 | 20.9 |
| Total | 2314 | 2.8 | 1.7 | 4.5 | 37.4 |

*INCOME, LAND OWNERSHIP, AND CHILD MORTALITY*

There is considerable variation in child mortality among couples distinguished by the husband's annual income. According to Table 99, the percentage of children claimed by death ranges from 43.5 for those earning less than 500 rupees to 20.9 for those earning 2000 rupees or more. Because of its low child mortality, the latter group, although not very fertile, has more living children, on the average, than any other income group. Conversely, those earning less than 500 rupees are quite fertile but have the smallest average number of living children. There are also variations in child mortality among couples distinguished by land ownership. As Table 100 shows, the

TABLE 100

Fertility and Child Mortality Among Couples Classified by Land Ownership

| LAND OWNERSHIP (IN ACRES) | NUMBER OF COUPLES | MEAN NUMBER OF CHILDREN | | | CHILD MORTALITY (PER CENT) |
|---|---|---|---|---|---|
| | | Living | Deceased | Ever Born | |
| None | 1308 | 2.8 | 1.7 | 4.5 | 37.8 |
| 1–9 | 403 | 2.5 | 1.8 | 4.3 | 41.9 |
| 10–19 | 297 | 3.0 | 1.6 | 4.6 | 34.8 |
| 20 or more | 306 | 3.4 | 1.4 | 4.8 | 29.2 |
| Total | 2314 | 2.8 | 1.7 | 4.5 | 37.4 |

110

percentage of children claimed by death is 41.9 for small owners (1–9 acres), 37.8 for the landless, 34.8 for medium owners (10–19 acres), and 29.2 for large owners (20 acres or more). Inspection of columns 5 and 6 indicates that child mortality declines as one moves from the least fertile to the most fertile group. Consequently, land ownership groups differ more in their average number of living children than in mean fertility.

*EDUCATION AND CHILD MORTALITY*

Table 101 presents the prevalence of child mortality among couples distinguished by the husband's educational achievement. The percentage of children claimed by death is 40.4 for the uneducated, 40.0

TABLE 101
Fertility and Child Mortality Among Classified by Education of Husband

| EDUCATION OF HUSBAND | NUMBER OF COUPLES | MEAN NUMBER OF CHILDREN | | | CHILD MORTALITY (PER CENT) |
|---|---|---|---|---|---|
| | | Living | Deceased | Ever Born | |
| None | 891 | 2.8 | 1.9 | 4.7 | 40.4 |
| Primary | 736 | 2.7 | 1.8 | 4.5 | 40.0 |
| Middle | 302 | 2.8 | 1.5 | 4.3 | 34.9 |
| High | 86 | 3.0 | 0.9 | 3.9 | 23.1 |
| Matriculation | 168 | 3.3 | 1.0 | 4.3 | 23.3 |
| College | 131 | 2.9 | 1.1 | 4.0 | 27.5 |
| Total | 2314 | 2.8 | 1.7 | 4.5 | 37.4 |

for the primary school educates, 34.9 for middle school educates, 23.1 for high school educates, 23.3 for matriculates, and 27.5 for the college group. The high school educates are the least fertile of all educational strata but because of low child mortality they are exceeded by only matriculates in the average number of living children. Conversely, the uneducated are the most fertile group but their average number of living children exceeds that of only primary school educates.

Child mortality also varies among couples distinguished by the wife's educational achievement. As Table 102 shows, the percentage of children claimed by death is 39.1 for the uneducated, 34.0 for the primary school group, and only 23.7 for those with more than primary school education  These with more than primary school education are much less fertile than the others but, because of their very low child mortality, their average number of living children is larger than that of the uneducated and only slightly lower than that of primary school educates.

TABLE 102

Fertility and Child Mortality Among Couples Classified by Education of Wife

| EDUCATION OF WIFE | NUMBER OF COUPLES | MEAN NUMBER OF CHILDREN Living | Deceased | Ever Born | CHILD MORTALITY (PER CENT) |
|---|---|---|---|---|---|
| None | 1772 | 2.8 | 1.8 | 4.6 | 39.1 |
| Primary | 318 | 3.1 | 1.6 | 4.7 | 34.0 |
| Above Primary | 224 | 2.9 | 0.9 | 3.8 | 23.7 |
| Total | 2314 | 2.8 | 1.7 | 4.5 | 37.4 |

## SUMMARY

The 2314 couples in our study gave birth to a total of 10,441 offspring.  At the time of the survey, 6537 (62.6 per cent) of them were still living and 3904 (37.4 per cent) of them had died.  Although we did not obtain information on the exact age at which each death occurred, it is evident from the rates of child mortality among couples in different age groups that almost all of the deaths occurred before age ten.  Because of the mortality factor, the average number of children to whom couples must give care and support is reduced from 4.5 to 2.8.

There is considerable variation among the various socio-economic strata in their rates of child mortality.  The most fertile groups ordinarily have an excessive amount and, consequently, they are growing in size more slowly than groups of quite low fertility.

# Interest in Birth Control and Socio-Economic Status

AT present, as the previous chapter shows, a high rate of child mortality reduces considerably the potential size of population in Central India. In the future, however, the influence of child mortality on population growth is expected to be much less because of public health and sanitation programs which the Government of India has introduced to control malaria, gastro-intestinal ailments, and other major causes of death. In view of this, many governmental officials and demographers feel that a rapid increase in population can be averted only by a greater use by married couples of contraceptives, sexual abstinence, and other techniques for limiting fertility. The use of these techniques is, of course, dependent upon both having knowledge of them and being motivated strongly to limit family size. It is, therefore, the purpose of this chapter to reveal the extent to which couples in Central India are aware of birth control techniques and are interested in family limitation.

Information on these topics was obtained during our survey by asking each couple a number of direct questions on birth control toward the end of the interview. The questions covered the following topics: present or past use of birth control techniques; knowledge of birth control techniques; interest in obtaining information on birth control techniques; interest in family limitation; and reasons for the interest in family limitation. In the case of couples who had completed their reproductive life—those over 45 years of age—questions were phrased with reference to their past rather than present situation. For example, they were asked, "were you ever interested in family limitation?" rather than "are you interested in family limitation?" The couples were generally cooperative but a few of them were obviously puzzled by the set of questions and answered after considerable hesitation.

113

## GENERAL FINDINGS

### *KNOWLEDGE OF BIRTH CONTROL TECHNIQUES*

Altogether 779 or 33.7 per cent of the 2314 couples in our study said that they knew some techniques by which births could be limited. When asked about the technique which they understood best, 402 of

TABLE 103

Percentage of Couples Having Knowledge of Birth Control Techniques, by Age of Wife

| KNOWLEDGE OF BIRTH CONTROL TECHNIQUES | PERCENTAGE OF COUPLES BY AGE OF WIFE | | | | |
|---|---|---|---|---|---|
| | Under 25 years (506)* | 25–34 years (778)* | 35–44 years (564)* | 45 years or more (466)* | Total (2314)* |
| Some | 37.1 | 37.0 | 31.2 | 27.2 | 33.7 |
| None | 62.9 | 63.0 | 68.8 | 72.8 | 66.3 |
| Total | 100.0 | 100.0 | 100.0 | 100.0 | 100.0 |

* The figures in parentheses in this table and subsequent tables refer to the number of couples.

the 779 couples mentioned sterilization, a technique which has been highly publicized by health centers in and around Nagpur City. Of the remaining couples, 215 mentioned sexual abstinence, the rhythm method, or *coitus interruptus*; 128 mentioned contraceptives; and six mentioned abortion. In addition, there are 28 couples who mentioned a variety of other techniques, some of which are ineffective as preventives of conception or birth. These include the use of various herbs and ayurvedic medicines, the placing of hot pads on the woman's stomach, the placing of pills in the vagina a half-hour before sexual intercourse, and the regulation of diet. The regulation of diet is usually connected with selfcontrol or abstinence, as indicated by the statement of one couple: "The size of the family can be controlled. Follow the rules of Jainism and avoid flesh, fish, salt, and mirchi (chili). These things make a man very hot and a hot man cannot control his mind and sexual feeling. That's why Gandhiji did not eat Masala (spicy) food."

114

Some of the couples who mentioned sterilization, contraceptives, and the rhythm method did not clearly understand these techniques. For example, some couples talked about the rhythm method and thought that the "danger period" was either three days preceding and the seven days following menses, the five days following menses, or the even days of the month.

*DESIRE FOR INFORMATION ON BIRTH CONTROL TECHNIQUES*

The 1535 couples who did not have knowledge of birth control techniques were asked whether they were now interested or had ever been interested in receiving information on them. Only 17.6 per cent

TABLE 104

Percentage of Couples Not Knowing of Birth Control Techniques Who Ever Desired Information on Them, by Age of Wife

| DESIRE FOR INFORMATION ON TECHNIQUES | PERCENTAGE OF COUPLES BY AGE OF WIFE | | | | |
|---|---|---|---|---|---|
| | Under 25 years (318) | 25–34 years (490) | 35–44 years (388) | 45 years or more (339) | Total (1535) |
| Some | 18.5 | 21.2 | 17.5 | 11.5 | 17.6 |
| None | 81.5 | 78.8 | 82.5 | 88.5 | 82.4 |
| Total | 100.0 | 100.0 | 100.0 | 100.0 | 100.0 |

of these couples responded in the affirmative. But even some of these were merely curious about the techniques rather than interested in family limitation. The small number of persons requesting information stems from two factors: first, a lack of interest in fertility control; and, secondly, an inability or unwillingness to imagine human control over fertility.

*USE OF BIRTH CONTROL TECHNIQUES*

As we noted in Chapter Five, only 127 couples said that they had ever used any technique to limit fertility. The major techniques used were: the rhythm method, *coitus interruptus*, or sexual abstinence in 64 instances; contraceptives in 35 instances; abortion in one instance; and undefined methods in two instances. In the remaining 25 cases, either the husband or wife, but usually the latter, had been sterilized.

TABLE 105
Percentage of Couples Who Ever Used Birth Control Techniques, by Age of Wife

| USE OF BIRTH CONTROL TECHNIQUES | PERCENTAGE OF COUPLES BY AGE OF WIFE | | | | Total (2314) |
|---|---|---|---|---|---|
| | Under 25 years (506) | 25–34 years (778) | 35–44 years (564) | 45 years or more (466) | |
| Never | 96.2 | 92.3 | 95.7 | 94.8 | 94.5 |
| Ever | 3.8 | 7.7 | 4.3 | 5.2 | 5.5 |
| Total | 100.0 | 100.0 | 100.0 | 100.0 | 100.0 |

Sterilization was, therefore, used by 6.2 per cent (25/402) of the couples knowing this technique. On the other hand, as Table 106 shows, contraceptives and sexual abstinence were used by over a quarter of the couples having knowledge of them.

The 127 couples using a technique constitute only 5.5 per cent of the total couples and only 16.3 per cent of the couples claiming knowledge of a technique. These figures are not, however, an adequate measure of the number of couples who will eventually use birth control techniques. Many of the knowledgeable couples said that they planned to abstain from cohabitation, or use contraceptives, or undergo sterilization once they had the number of children which they desire. Others said that they were interested in limiting their

TABLE 106
Relation Between Knowledge and Use of Various Birth Control Techniques

| KNOWLEDGE OF | NUMBER OF COUPLES | | | PERCENTAGE OF COUPLES | | |
|---|---|---|---|---|---|---|
| | Non-Use | Use | Total | Non-Use | Use | Total |
| Abstinence* | 151 | 64 | 215 | 70.2 | 29.8 | 100.0 |
| Abortion | 5 | 1 | 6 | 83.3 | 16.7 | 100.0 |
| Sterilization | 377 | 25 | 402 | 93.8 | 6.2 | 100.0 |
| Contraceptives | 93 | 35 | 128 | 72.7 | 27.3 | 100.0 |
| Other | 26 | 2 | 28 | 92.9 | 7.1 | 100.0 |
| Total | 652 | 127 | 779 | 83.7 | 16.3 | 100.0 |

* Includes the rhythm method and *coitus interruptus*.

116

fertility but hesitated to use the birth control technique which they knew because of either its unreliability or its harmful consequences. The following statement by one couple is rather representative of the views of those who felt that sterilization was harmful.

"Family planning is very essential. But the means [sterilization] are very harmful; sometimes they are savage. They are profitable but in the long run they are harmful. If proper rest is not given to the woman she loses her health as well as charm in life. If she becomes a widow and is willing to remarry, she can't marry because she is sterilized. So sometimes this [sterilization] is very harmful."

Other couples who planned to limit their fertility said that they objected to contraceptives, sterilization, and *coitus interruptus* on religious and moral grounds. They planned to control fertility by abstaining from sexual activity but would first have to undergo the required disciplinary training. As the following statement indicates, abstinence is not offensive to moral sentiments, but quite the contrary.

"I don't like birth control devices. They prevent the natural growth of humanity. But mental restriction is a good way and there is a moral appeal to it. Man should study at least this. God is always doing some experiment in man. Prevention of overpopulation requires the study of mental restriction, not the use of devices. At least man shows God that he can do this much as a service to society."

### INTEREST IN FAMILY LIMITATION

The desire for a limited number of children was expressed by 1626 couples or 70.3 per cent of the total couples. Of those having this interest, 912 either had knowledge of birth control techniques or requested information on them. But, as we pointed out previously, the willingness to use these techniques depends on health, religious, moral, and practical considerations. The other 714 couples had neither a knowledge of nor a desire for information on birth control techniques. They strongly believed that only God could fulfill their desire for a limited number of children. This viewpoint was aptly expressed by a couple who said that they wanted no more than five children.

"We cannot control the growth of children. Can we control the growth of trees in the forest? Like that, we are trees in this forest of

TABLE 107

Percentage of Couples Interested in Family Limitation Who Have
Knowledge of Birth Control Techniques

| KNOWLEDGE OF BIRTH CONTROL TECHNIQUES | PERCENTAGE OF COUPLES | | Total (2314) |
|---|---|---|---|
| | Interested in Family Limitation (1626) | Not Interested in Family Limitation (788) | |
| Present | 42.8 | 12.1 | 33.7 |
| Desired | 13.3 | 7.7 | 11.6 |
| Absent and Not Desired | 43.9 | 80.2 | 54.7 |
| Total | 100.0 | 100.0 | 100.0 |

the world. God will come and cut down some trees. If God feels
that he wants to limit the size of a particular family, he can do so. He
has got the account of humanity. Man cannot control."

Interest in family limitation varies among couples distinguished by
the number of living children. According to Table 108, the interest is
strongest among the childless couples and weakest among the most

TABLE 108

Distribution of Couples by Number of Living Children
and Interest in Family Limitation

| NUMBER OF LIVING CHILDREN | NUMBER OF COUPLES | PERCENTAGE OF COUPLES | | Total |
|---|---|---|---|---|
| | | No Interest in Family Limitation | Some Interest in Family Limitation | |
| 0 | 314 | 25.4 | 74.6 | 100.0 |
| 1 | 429 | 28.4 | 71.6 | 100.0 |
| 2 | 414 | 29.8 | 70.2 | 100.0 |
| 3 | 387 | 29.8 | 70.2 | 100.0 |
| 4 | 282 | 30.4 | 69.6 | 100.0 |
| 5 | 210 | 29.8 | 70.2 | 100.0 |
| 6 | 148 | 32.6 | 67.4 | 100.0 |
| 7 | 59 | 44.1 | 55.9 | 100.0 |
| 8 | 37 | 35.0 | 65.0 | 100.0 |
| 9 | 19 | 38.0 | 61.9 | 100.0 |
| 10 or more | 15 | 50.0 | 50.0 | 100.0 |
| Total | 2314 | 29.7 | 70.3 | 100.0 |

118

fertile couples. But the interest in family limitation does not decline regularly as the number of living children increases. For example, couples having seven children are less interested than are those having eight or nine children.

Interest in family limitation varies among couples distinguished by the wife's age. According to Table 109, the percentage of couples ever interested in family limitation is 77.1 for those under 25 years of

TABLE 109
Percentage of Couples Ever Interested in
Family Limitation, by Age of Wife

| INTEREST IN FAMILY LIMITATION | PERCENTAGE OF COUPLES BY AGE OF WIFE | | | | |
|---|---|---|---|---|---|
| | Under 25 years (506) | 25–34 years (778) | 35–44 years (564) | 45 years or more (466) | Total (2314) |
| Some | 77.1 | 71.8 | 67.1 | 62.1 | 70.3 |
| None | 22.9 | 28.2 | 32.9 | 37.9 | 29.7 |
| Total | 100.0 | 100.0 | 100.0 | 100.0 | 100.0 |

age, 71.8 for those 25–34 years old, 67.1 for those 35–44 years old, and 62.1 for those 45 or more years of age. The fact that the young couples, who are just beginning their reproductive lives, are most interested in family limitation is of great practical significance.

*INTEREST IN FAMILY LIMITATION AND IDEAL NUMBER OF CHILDREN*

The couples who expressed an interest in family limitation were asked to indicate the number of children which they consider ideal. Their responses are presented in Table 110. Over half of the couples said that they wanted either three or four children, and over three-quarters of them wanted from two to five children. In most cases, the ideal number is not greatly influenced by the number of living children which couples have. For example, of the 284 couples who indicated that two children would be ideal, 106 have fewer than two living children, 75 have two living children, and 103 have more than two living children. The effect of age on the ideal number of children is shown in Table 111.

119

TABLE 110

Relation Between Number of Living Children and Ideal Number of Children for Couples Interested in Family Limitation

| IDEAL NUMBER OF CHILDREN | NUMBER OF LIVING CHILDREN | | | | | | | | | | | TOTAL COUPLES |
|---|---|---|---|---|---|---|---|---|---|---|---|---|
| | 0 | 1 | 2 | 3 | 4 | 5 | 6 | 7 | 8 | 9 | 10 or more | |
| 0 | 4 | 3 | 3 | 2 | 1 | 2 | 2 | — | — | — | — | 17 |
| 1 | 13 | 19 | 4 | 2 | 2 | 1 | 1 | — | — | — | — | 42 |
| 2 | 50 | 56 | 75 | 37 | 32 | 15 | 12 | 1 | 4 | 2 | — | 284 |
| 3 | 58 | 80 | 68 | 72 | 34 | 26 | 17 | 7 | 4 | 2 | 1 | 369 |
| 4 | 76 | 88 | 92 | 88 | 79 | 39 | 29 | 10 | 7 | 5 | 1 | 514 |
| 5 | 15 | 39 | 25 | 45 | 25 | 31 | 9 | 4 | 2 | — | — | 195 |
| 6 | 9 | 8 | 22 | 14 | 16 | 11 | 22 | 4 | 6 | 1 | ·2 | 115 |
| 7–9 | 7 | 12 | 9 | 11 | 8 | 21 | 5 | 7 | 3 | 3 | 4 | 90 |
| Total Couples | 232 | 305 | 298 | 271 | 197 | 146 | 97 | 33 | 26 | 13 | 8 | 1626 |
| Mean | 3.4 | 3.5 | 3.5 | 3.8 | 3.9 | 4.5 | 4.2 | 5.0 | 4.4 | 5.1 | 6.6 | 3.8 |

TABLE 111

Ideal Number of Children According to Couples Interested in Family Limitation, by Age of Wife

| IDEAL NUMBER OF CHILDREN | PERCENTAGE OF COUPLES BY AGE OF WIFE | | | | |
|---|---|---|---|---|---|
| | Under 25 years (393) | 25–34 years (562) | 35–44 years (380) | 45 years or more (291) | Total (1626) |
| 0 | 1.1 | 1.0 | — | 3.0 | 1.0 |
| 1 | 2.2 | 3.9 | 2.7 | 1.3 | 2.6 |
| 2 | 20.6 | 19.5 | 15.5 | 14.6 | 17.5 |
| 3 | 28.6 | 20.7 | 20.7 | 16.7 | 22.7 |
| 4 | 33.7 | 28.9 | 31.1 | 36.5 | 31.6 |
| 5 | 8.9 | 16.0 | 10.7 | 9.0 | 12.0 |
| 6 | 3.8 | 6.1 | 11.9 | 7.7 | 7.1 |
| 7–9 | 1.1 | 3.9 | 7.4 | 11.2 | 5.5 |
| Total | 100.0 | 100.0 | 100.0 | 100.0 | 100.0 |
| Mean | 3.4 | 3.7 | 4.1 | 4.2 | 3.7 |

120

The reasons why couples are interested or not interested in family limitation are also of considerable importance, and they are presented in the last part of this chapter. At this point, consideration can be given to the variations among socio-economic strata in their knowledge of birth control techniques as well as interest in family limitation.

## SOCIO-ECONOMIC PATTERNS

### RESIDENCE AND BIRTH CONTROL

According to Table 112, both the knowledge of techniques and the interest in family limitation varies according to place of residence. The percentage of knowledgeable couples is 46.6 in the city, 27.8 in

ILE 112

entage of Couples Having Knowledge of Birth Control Techniques and ested in Family Limitation, by Residence

| Residence | Number of Couples | KNOWLEDGE | | | INTEREST | | |
|---|---|---|---|---|---|---|---|
| | | Some | None | Total | Some | None | Total |
| City | 882 | 46.6 | 53.4 | 100.0 | 78.4 | 21.6 | 100.0 |
| Town | 309 | 27.8 | 72.2 | 100.0 | 72.2 | 27.8 | 100.0 |
| Village | 1123 | 25.1 | 74.9 | 100.0 | 64.0 | 36.0 | 100.0 |
| Total | 2314 | 33.7 | 66.3 | 100.0 | 70.3 | 29.7 | 100.0 |

the towns, and 25.1 in the villages. The interest in the family limitation is also greatest in the city and least in the villages, but residential groups differ less in this respect than they do in their knowledge of techniques.

### RELIGION, CASTE, AND BIRTH CONTROL

Table 113 presents the relation between religion and knowledge of techniques and interest in family limitation. The percentage of knowledgeable couples is 32.1 for Hindus, 31.6 for Buddhists, 54.6 for Muslims, and 57.9 for "Other Religions" (Christians, Sikhs, Jains, and Parsees). Interest in limitation was expressed by 69.2 per cent of the Hindus, 67.4 per cent of the Buddhists, 83.3 per cent of the Muslims, and 87.5 per cent of the "Other Religions."

TABLE 113

Percentage of Couples Having Knowledge of Birth Control Techniques and Interested in Family Limitation, by Religion

| | Number of Couples | Percentage of Couples | | | | | |
|---|---|---|---|---|---|---|---|
| | | KNOWLEDGE | | | INTEREST | | |
| Religion | | Some | None | Total | Some | None | Total |
| Hindu | 1923 | 32.1 | 67.9 | 100.0 | 69.2 | 30.8 | 100. |
| Buddhist | 237 | 31.6 | 68.4 | 100.0 | 67.4 | 32.6 | 100. |
| Muslim | 97 | 54.6 | 45.4 | 100.0 | 83.3 | 16.7 | 100. |
| Other | 57 | 57.9 | 42.1 | 100.0 | 87.5 | 12.5 | 100. |
| Total | 2314 | 33.7 | 66.3 | 100.0 | 70.3 | 29.7 | 100. |

TABLE 114

Percentage of Couples Having Knowledge of Birth Control Techniques and Interested in Family Limitation, by Caste

| | Number of Couples | Percentage of Couples | | | | | |
|---|---|---|---|---|---|---|---|
| | | KNOWLEDGE | | | INTEREST | | |
| Caste | | Some | None | Total | Some | None | Total |
| Brahmin | 215 | 65.6 | 34.4 | 100.0 | 90.0 | 10.0 | 100. |
| Maratha | 57 | 43.9 | 56.1 | 100.0 | 91.7 | 8.3 | 100. |
| Kunbi | 400 | 24.8 | 75.2 | 100.0 | 61.0 | 39.0 | 100. |
| Mali | 124 | 27.4 | 72.6 | 100.0 | 65.6 | 34.4 | 100 |
| Bania and other trading castes | 82 | 47.6 | 52.4 | 100.0 | 76.0 | 24.0 | 100. |
| Kosthi | 158 | 11.4 | 88.6 | 100.0 | 54.8 | 45.2 | 100. |
| Sonar, Lohar and other artisan castes | 118 | 32.2 | 67.8 | 100.0 | 71.6 | 28.4 | 100. |
| Teli | 212 | 23.6 | 76.4 | 100.0 | 69.7 | 30.3 | 100. |
| Dhobi, Nai and other service castes | 141 | 22.0 | 78.0 | 100.0 | 67.5 | 32.5 | 100. |
| Scheduled castes | | | | | | | |
| Mahar | 130 | 30.8 | 69.2 | 100.0 | 66.7 | 33.3 | 100. |
| Other | 68 | 17.6 | 82.4 | 100.0 | 55.6 | 44.4 | 100. |
| Gond | 50 | 4.0 | 96.0 | 100.0 | 55.1 | 44.9 | 100. |
| Other | 168 | 53.5 | 46.5 | 100.0 | 77.1 | 22.9 | 100. |
| Total Hindus | 1923 | 32.1 | 67.9 | 100.0 | 69.2 | 30.8 | 100. |

122

Considerable variation is also present among Hindus differentiated by caste membership. According to Table 114, 65.6 per cent of the Brahmins but only 11.4 per cent of the Kosthis and only 4.0 per cent of the Gonds have knowledge of any birth control technique. However, over half of the Kosthis and Gonds are interested in family limitation. In the case of the remaining castes, the percentage of couples interested in limitation ranges from 55.6 for Scheduled Castes (excluding Mahars) to 90.0 for Brahmins and 91.7 for Marathas.

*OCCUPATION AND BIRTH CONTROL*

Couples who are differentiated by the husband's occupation also differ in their knowledge of techniques and interest in limitation.

According to Table 115, the percentage of knowledgeable couples ranges from 20.2 for the unskilled to 65.1 for the professionals. The professionals are also the group having the greatest interest in family limitation. Whereas 91.9 per cent of them expressed such interest, only 62.4 per cent of the agriculturalists and 62.6 per cent of the unskilled did so.

The knowledge of techniques and interest in limitation also vary slightly when couples are classified by the wife's employment rather than the husband's. According to Table 116, 34.6 per cent of the

.BLE 115

centage of Couples Having Knowledge of Birth Control Techniques and erested in Family Limitation, by Occupation of Husband*

| Occupational Group | Number of Couples | Percentage of Couples | | | | | |
| --- | --- | --- | --- | --- | --- | --- | --- |
| | | KNOWLEDGE | | | INTEREST | | |
| | | Some | None | Total | Some | None | Total |
| skilled | 272 | 20.2 | 79.8 | 100.0 | 62.6 | 37.4 | 100.0 |
| isan | 629 | 27.3 | 72.7 | 100.0 | 70.0 | 30.0 | 100.0 |
| de | 326 | 36.2 | 63.8 | 100.0 | 68.9 | 31.1 | 100.0 |
| rical | 198 | 58.6 | 41.4 | 100.0 | 86.4 | 13.6 | 100.0 |
| fessional and administrative | 249 | 65.1 | 34.9 | 100.0 | 91.9 | 8.1 | 100.0 |
| ricultural | 611 | 23.9 | 76.1 | 100.0 | 62.4 | 37.6 | 100.0 |
| al | 2285 | 33.7 | 66.3 | 100.0 | 70.3 | 29.7 | 100.0 |

Excludes 29 couples where the husband was unemployed.

TABLE 116

Percentage of Couples Having Knowledge of Birth Control Techniques and Interested in Family Limitation, by Employment Status of Wife

| Employment Status | Number of Couples | Percentage of Couples | | | | | |
| | | KNOWLEDGE | | | INTEREST | | |
| | | Some | None | Total | Some | None | Total |
|---|---|---|---|---|---|---|---|
| Unemployed | 2035 | 34.6 | 65.4 | 100.0 | 70.8 | 29.2 | 100 |
| Employed | 279 | 26.5 | 73.5 | 100.0 | 67.0 | 33.0 | 100 |
| Total | 2314 | 33.7 | 66.3 | 100.0 | 70.3 | 29.7 | 100 |

unemployed and 26.5 per cent of the employed have knowledge of some technique. There is very little difference between the groups in their interest in family limitation, the percentage of interested couples being 70.8 for the unemployed and 67.0 for the employed.

*INCOME, LAND OWNERSHIP, AND BIRTH CONTROL*

Table 117 presents the relation between husband's annual income and the knowledge of techniques and interest in family limitation. The percentage of knowledgeable couples ranges from 17.8 for those earning less than 500 rupees to 66.9 for those earning 1500–1999 rupees. Interest in family limitation was expressed by 57.6 per cent of those earning less than 500 rupees, 66.4 per cent of those earning

TABLE 117

Percentage of Couples Having Knowledge of Birth Control Techniques and Interested in Family Limitation, by Annual Income of Husband

| Annual Income (in rupees) | Number of Couples | Percentage of Couples | | | | | |
| | | KNOWLEDGE | | | INTEREST | | |
| | | Some | None | Total | Some | None | Total |
|---|---|---|---|---|---|---|---|
| Under 500 | 650 | 17.8 | 82.2 | 100.0 | 57.6 | 42.4 | 100 |
| 500– 999 | 877 | 27.9 | 72.1 | 100.0 | 66.4 | 33.6 | 100 |
| 1000–1499 | 360 | 43.3 | 56.7 | 100.0 | 81.9 | 18.1 | 100 |
| 1500–1999 | 124 | 66.9 | 33.1 | 100.0 | 82.7 | 17.3 | 100 |
| 2000 and over | 303 | 59.1 | 40.9 | 100.0 | 83.9 | 16.1 | 100 |
| Total | 2314 | 33.7 | 66.3 | 100.0 | 70.3 | 29.7 | 100 |

124

500–999 rupees, and by slightly over 80.0 per cent of the other three income groups.

There is little variation among land ownership groups in their knowledge of techniques and interest in family limitation. According to Table 118, the percentage of knowledgeable couples ranges from 26.6 for the small owners (1–9 acres) to 38.9 for the large owners (20 acres or more). The percentage of couples interested in family limitation ranges from 69.2 for the landless group to 75.8 for the large owners.

BLE 118

centage of Couples Having Knowledge of Birth Control Techniques and erested in Family Limitation, by Land Ownership

| Land Ownership (in acres) | Number of Couples | Percentage of Couples | | | | | |
| | | KNOWLEDGE | | | INTEREST | | |
| | | Some | None | Total | Some | None | Total |
|---|---|---|---|---|---|---|---|
| None | 1308 | 35.3 | 64.7 | 100.0 | 69.2 | 30.8 | 100.0 |
| 1–9 | 403 | 26.6 | 73.4 | 100.0 | 72.2 | 27.8 | 100.0 |
| 10–19 | 297 | 30.6 | 69.4 | 100.0 | 70.5 | 29.5 | 100.0 |
| 20 and over | 306 | 38.9 | 61.1 | 100.0 | 75.8 | 24.2 | 100.0 |
| Total | 2314 | 33.7 | 66.3 | 100.0 | 70.3 | 29.7 | 100.0 |

## EDUCATION AND BIRTH CONTROL

Couples who are distinguished by the husband's educational achievement differ greatly in their knowledge of techniques and interest in family limitation. According to Table 119, the percentage of knowledgeable couples ranges from 16.4 for the uneducated to 85.5 for the college trained. There is, in fact, a regular rise in the knowledge of birth control techniques as education increases. The degree to which couples are interested in limitation also corresponds closely with educational attainment. This interest was expressed by 56.1 per cent of the uneducated and by 95.7 per cent of the college trained.

When couples are classified by the wife's educational achievement, both the knowledge of techniques and the interest in family limitation are found to be positively associated with higher education. The

TABLE 119

Percentage of Couples Having Knowledge of Birth Control Techniques and Interested in Family Limitation, by Education of Husband

| Educational Level | Number of Couples | Percentage of Couples | | | | | |
|---|---|---|---|---|---|---|---|
| | | KNOWLEDGE | | | INTEREST | | |
| | | Some | None | Total | Some | None | To |
| None | 891 | 16.4 | 83.6 | 100.0 | 56.1 | 43.9 | 100 |
| Primary | 736 | 31.4 | 68.6 | 100.0 | 74.5 | 25.5 | 100 |
| Middle | 302 | 42.4 | 57.6 | 100.0 | 72.0 | 28.0 | 100 |
| High | 86 | 54.7 | 45.3 | 100.0 | 86.8 | 13.2 | 100 |
| Matriculation | 168 | 68.4 | 31.6 | 100.0 | 89.8 | 10.2 | 100 |
| College | 131 | 85.5 | 14.5 | 100.0 | 95.7 | 4.3 | 100 |
| Total | 2314 | 33.7 | 66.3 | 100.0 | 70.3 | 29.7 | 100 |

TABLE 120

Percentage of Couples Having Knowledge of Birth Control Techniques and Interested in Family Limitation, by Education of Wife

| Educational Level | Number of Couples | Percentage of Couples | | | | | |
|---|---|---|---|---|---|---|---|
| | | KNOWLEDGE | | | INTEREST | | |
| | | Some | None | Total | Some | None | Tot |
| None | 1772 | 23.7 | 76.3 | 100.0 | 63.9 | 36.1 | 100. |
| Primary | 318 | 59.1 | 40.9 | 100.0 | 83.0 | 17.0 | 100. |
| Above Primary | 224 | 76.3 | 23.7 | 100.0 | 95.5 | 4.5 | 100. |
| Total | 2314 | 33.7 | 66.3 | 100.0 | 70.3 | 29.7 | 100. |

percentage of knowledgeable couples is 23.7 for the uneducated, 59.1 for those with primary schooling, and 76.3 for those with more than primary schooling. Interest in limitation was expressed by 63.9 per cent of the uneducated, 83.0 per cent of those with primary schooling, and 95.5 per cent of those with more than primary schooling.

## FACTORS AFFECTING INTEREST IN FAMILY LIMITATION

It was pointed out earlier in this chapter that 1626 couples expressed an interest in family limitation and that 688 couples were opposed to it. In this section, attention is given to the various reasons why couples favored or opposed a limited number of children.

### OPPOSITION TO FAMILY LIMITATION

The major reasons given by couples for their opposition to a limited number of children were usually religious or economic ones. The majority—356 couples—stressed the ideas that "children are God's gifts" and that "only God can control the processes of birth and death." They cited as proof of this the fact that some couples have many children and others are childless after many years of married life. The number of children which a couple has is viewed as a sign of God's blessing or curse. One couple expressed this view as follows:

"Everyone is not blessed generously by the God. Many persons do not get even one child. I know a person who married seven times—one marriage after the other—for the sake of obtaining children but he was never blessed with one child. We ourselves were much disappointed when we were without any issue for about 20 years after marriage. It was natural birth control to us. But Almighty has given us, though in our old age, one child. We are bound by our destinies."

Twelve couples were opposed to family limitation because they felt that natural controls now operated to ensure a small number of children. Five of them said that they and their parents had had relatively few offspring after many years of marriage and suggested that they were biologically incapable of conceiving often. Six others who were much more fertile said that they wanted as many children as possible because over half of the children born to them had already died and they had no guarantee that the remaining ones would live beyond childhood. The last couple looked at matters from a societal rather than a personal perspective and argued that natural checks are now operating to control the growth of population: "Human beings cannot control the growth of humanity. Of course man plays a prominent role in moulding the career of a child. It does not mean that he can limit the size of population. Population is reduced by wars. Wars and epidemics are nature's own check, not man's. The methods invented by Nature reduce the ever increasing population."

There are 115 couples who gave some economic reason for not being interested in family limitation. Thirteen of them said that they weren't interested because they had sufficient income and other resources to provide adequate food, shelter, clothing, medical care, and education for any number of children. Forty couples said that their resources were few but nevertheless they were not interested in family limitation. They felt that the government had an obligation to ease the economic pressure upon them by increasing opportunities for employment and higher wages, and by providing subsidies for couples with a large number of children.

The other 62 couples viewed a large number of children as a definite economic asset. Those engaged in weaving, cultivation and business said that all children could be of assistance to the parents in their work and that the prosperity of the family depends upon its size. Those engaged in other occupations said a large number of children would assure the parents of having someone to give them care and support when they were aged or infirm. Some couples of various occupational backgrounds pointed out that they had several daughters and wanted as many sons as possible because this would be economically advantageous when it came time to get the children married. As several couples put it, "daughters are the wealth of others, so we must have more sons. Marriage in the case of girls is very expensive—money goes out whereas in the case of boys it is just the opposite."

Of the remaining 205 couples, 34 were not interested in family limitation because either a large family is traditional, children are a source of great pleasure to the parents, large families are a source of prestige and power in the community; a large family is much more harmonious than a small one; and the physical and psychological health of the mother is fostered by her giving birth to many offspring. The other 171 couples were unable to give any reason for their opposition to family limitation.

*INTEREST IN LIMITATION*

The 1626 couples who favored family limitation gave various reasons for their attitude. The majority—1120 couples—were interested because of economic factors. Of these, 745 couples said that

128

their earnings were so low and prices so high that they found it difficult to provide their children with the bare essentials—food, shelter and clothing. One hundred and three other couples, who were in a better economic position, favored limitation in order that they might achieve or maintain a comfortable standard of living. The remaining 272 couples were able to manage quite well at present but were greatly concerned about the expenses which they would have when their children entered college and then, possibly, a professional school. They felt that parents were strongly obliged to provide whatever finances were necessary for their children's achievement.

Forty-eight couples gave a health reason for favoring family limitation. They pointed out that the mother's health is injured by frequent deliveries and by bearing children after her youth has passed. The health of the father may also be affected by a large number of children. In the words of one couple, "too many children affect the mother's health and also the father's. He must work harder and harder to support them and thus his health is reduced day by day."

Of the remaining couples, 169 favored limitation for one of the following reasons: a small family is more affectionate and functions smoothly; parents can easily control a small number of children; it is more easy to divide property and provide an adequate inheritance for a small number of children; one can easily arrange proper marriages for a small number of children, especially girls; the number of sons desired have been born and are healthy; and it is a patriotic duty to limit the number of children. In the words of one couple: "Population in our country is increasing very fast. It is our duty to help the Government in controlling the population. If we are not in a position to maintain our children we should check their birth. I am not in a position to maintain a big family. After two or three births I will get my wife operated [sterilized]. It is better for me and my country."

Lastly, there are 42 couples who felt that it was sinful or immoral for parents to have children whose needs could not be adequately met, and 247 couples who failed to give any reason for their interest in family limitation.

## SUMMARY

At the present time, birth control techniques are not especially popular in Central India. They are known to about one third of all couples and they have been used occasionally by about five per cent of them. The couples who have no knowledge of any of the techniques rarely expressed an interest in learning about them.

The general lack of knowledge of or interest in birth control devices does not mean that couples are not interested in family limitation. Altogether, 70.3 per cent of the total couples said that they wanted a small number of children because of economic or health considerations. There is, however, a strong feeling that fulfillment of this desire should or must stem from divine intervention. The couples who oppose family limitation usually say that they can support and educate a large number of children or that children are a sign of God's blessing.

There is considerable variation among the several socio-economic strata in their knowledge of birth control devices and interest in family limitation. This interest is strongest in the city and among couples belonging to the minority religions, the professional class, and the higher income and educational groups.

# General Summary

THE social structure of India has remained rather static over the past half-century but is now undergoing various changes because of recent social legislation, the Five-Year Plans, and several voluntary movements. These changes include, among others, modifications in the proportions of persons who are educated, living in urban areas, owning land, and employed in different occupational classes. The occupations whose representation in the total labor force is expected to increase most include: semi-skilled and skilled workers; engineers, doctors and nurses; rural extension workers; and managerial and administrative personnel. Income levels are also expected to change, providing a reduction in the proportion of persons now found in the low income groups. The proportions of the population who are landless and who have large holdings may be reduced by various land reform measures. Greater opportunities for primary and secondary schooling and the adult literacy campaign are expected to alter the ratio of illiterate persons to educated ones. In addition, shifts from Hinduism to Buddhism are occurring and the size of the scheduled caste population is being reduced by social and legal devices.

The general purpose of this study was to determine whether it is reasonable to assume that the above-mentioned changes in social structure will have any bearing on the general fertility rate. As we indicated in Chapter One, such an assumption could be reasonably made if two conditions are found to exist. First, it must be demonstrated that fertility varies among groups which are currently differentiated in social status. Secondly, it is necessary to demonstrate that the fertility of persons who shift from one status to another resembles that of the stratum in which they gain membership. This study which is based on a sample survey conducted in Central India has dealt with only the first of these two considerations. The second one was not handled because our sample was too small to permit the detailed classification and analysis which are necessary for a thorough examination of it.

131

Our inquiry has shown that several socio-economic strata do differ significantly in their fertility patterns whereas others do not. The patterns are quite similar for couples who are distinguished on the basis of either place of residence, occupational class, or income level. On the other hand, the patterns are dissimilar for couples who belong to either different religions, castes, land ownership groups, or educational levels. Of particular importance is the fact that fertility is especially high among the subgroups whose representation in the social structure is expected to be reduced by legal, economic, and social measures. These include, among others, the large land owners, the uneducated, and the scheduled castes.

There are a number of possible explanations of the differences among socio-economic strata in fertility. The differences may be attributed to various physical factors or cultural practices, or a combination of them, which determine how frequently groups are exposed to the risks of pregnancy. Among the physical or biological factors are sterility, prolonged illnesses or disabilities, the age at which widowhood occurs, and physical separation necessitated by employment. The cultural factors include the practice of the wife returning to the parental home for child delivery and prolonged postnatal care, the belief that frequent sexual intercourse is injurious to health, sexual abstinence during lactation and during long periods of religious observance, age at marriage, and the type of family structure to which couples belong after marriage.

We were unable to determine the relevance of all of these factors to fertility differentials but did ascertain the importance of several of them. The differences among socio-economic strata are unrelated to rates of widowhood or spinsterhood because of the nature of our inquiry. In the main it was based on couples rather than women of different marital statuses and therefore the matter of widowhood is not pertinent. Sterility may also be eliminated as an explanation of the fertility differences. According to our analyses the strata are very similar in their incidence of sterility, as measured by the number of childless couples. In addition to these two factors, three others were intensively examined in terms of their bearing on the fertility patterns.

This examination shows that the differentials are not accounted for by variations among the strata in their use of contraceptives and other birth control devices.  In fact, only a small percentage of the couples have knowledge of any technique which can be used to limit births.  Of those having such knowledge, only a few of them ever used a technique and most of them did so on an irregular basis or after the number of children had become excessive.  In the future, the use of birth control devices may play an important role in determining levels of fertility.  The majority of couples in every socio-economic stratum expressed a strong interest in family limitation, usually stating that they want no more than three or four children.  They were interested primarily because of either the harmful effect of many deliveries on the mother's health or the economic burden of supporting and giving care to many children.  It is highly probable that rising income levels will lower the economic motivation.  The majority of couples who were opposed to family limitation said that they were in a position to educate and give care to a large number of children.

This examination also shows that the type of family structure in which couples have membership does not account for the fertility differentials among socio-economic strata.  The strata do differ considerably in their ratios of joint-families to nuclear families but fertility is found to be independent of the type of family structure.  In view of this independence, the decline among all groups in joint-family living will have no bearing on the future course of fertility.

Lastly, differences among the strata in their ages at marriage were considered as a possible explanation of their variations in fertility.  This analysis revealed a slight positive association between young age at marriage and high fertility.  But the weakness of this association does not permit us to view differences in age at marriage as the explanation of the fertility differentials among socio-economic strata.

It is important to stress the fact that our findings pertain only to Central India.  They partly agree and partly disagree with the findings of studies conducted in other areas of India.  When all of the studies are compared, one finds that there is not for all areas of India any uniform relationship between fertility and religion, income, or any other dimension of socio-economic status.  As we noted in Chapter One, this lack of uniformity may in part be attributed to differences

133

among researchers in their methods of measuring fertility and defining dimensions of social status. But, differences in method are not the sole explanation. The Gokhale Institute employed approximately the same methods in analyzing fertility patterns in four districts of Western India but found that the relationship between fertility and certain dimensions of social status differed somewhat from one district to another. It would therefore seem that the kinds of fertility differentials which a researcher discovers in India will depend in part upon the area of study.

# Appendix 1

## The Classification of Castes

OUR analyses of the relation of caste to fertility and other characteristics were performed after the 1923 Hindu couples were divided up into thirteen caste groups. About two-thirds of the couples identified themselves as, and were thus classified as, either Brahmin, Maratha, Kunbi, Mali, Kosthi, Teli, Mahar, or Gond. The other one-third were distributed over more than one hundred specific castes. Each of these groups turned out to be numerically small and it was therefore necessary to combine them under broad headings such as Trading Castes or Artisan Castes. In order to make these combinations, we consulted the studies of Hutton (*Caste in India*), Ghurye (*Caste and Class in India*), and other experts to learn which castes are considered similar in social function and prestige.

| | NUMBER OF COUPLES | | | |
| CASTE GROUPS | City | Towns | Villages | Total |
|---|---|---|---|---|
| *Brahmin* | 165 | 7 | 43 | 215 |
| *Maratha* | 29 | 17 | 11 | 57 |
| *Kunbi* | 62 | 43 | 295 | 400 |
| *Mali* | 5 | 66 | 53 | 124 |
| *Trading Castes* | | | | |
|   Agarwal | 6 | — | — | 6 |
|   Chhatri | — | — | 2 | 2 |
|   Gujerati | 3 | 1 | — | 4 |
|   Halwai | 1 | — | — | 1 |
|   Jaiswal, oswal | 3 | 2 | — | 5 |
|   Javeri | 1 | — | — | 1 |
|   Khatri | 1 | 1 | 3 | 5 |

135

| CASTE GROUPS | NUMBER OF COUPLES | | | |
| --- | --- | --- | --- | --- |
| | City | Towns | Villages | Total |
| *Trading Castes (Continued)* | | | | |
| Kirad | 4 | — | — | 4 |
| Lohana | 3 | — | — | 3 |
| Marwari, bania | 12 | 1 | 8 | 21 |
| Sindhi | 9 | 1 | 13 | 23 |
| Vaish | 6 | — | — | 6 |
| Vani | 1 | — | — | 1 |
| Total | 50 | 6 | 26 | 82 |
| *Kosthi* | 42 | 39 | 77 | 158 |
| *Artisan Castes* | | | | |
| Badai, badhi | — | 1 | 2 | 3 |
| Barhai | 1 | — | — | 1 |
| Chatri | 1 | — | — | 1 |
| Kachwadi, Khachwadi | — | — | 2 | 2 |
| Kasar | 1 | — | 1 | 2 |
| Khati | — | — | 3 | 3 |
| Kumbhar | 3 | 4 | 4 | 11 |
| Kuredi | — | — | 1 | 1 |
| Lohar | 5 | 5 | 6 | 16 |
| Meddhi | — | 3 | — | 3 |
| Pancha | — | 2 | — | 2 |
| Shimpi, darzi | 6 | 4 | 13 | 23 |
| Sonar, soni | 19 | 5 | 4 | 28 |
| Sutar | 3 | 3 | 10 | 16 |
| Tambat | — | — | 1 | 1 |
| Wadi, wadhi | 1 | — | 4 | 5 |
| Total | 40 | 27 | 51 | 118 |
| *Teli* | 46 | 28 | 138 | 212 |
| *Service Castes* | | | | |
| Ahir, yadav | 9 | — | 1 | 10 |

## CLASSIFICATION OF CASTES

| CASTE GROUPS | NUMBER OF COUPLES | | | |
| --- | --- | --- | --- | --- |
| | City | Towns | Villages | Total |
| *Service Castes* (*continued*) | | | | |
| Barai | 4 | 1 | 1 | 6 |
| Beldar | — | — | 1 | 1 |
| Bhoi | 1 | 3 | 2 | 6 |
| Burad | — | 3 | — | 3 |
| Dhangar | 1 | 3 | 26 | 30 |
| Dhimar | 1 | 5 | 11 | 17 |
| Gaoli | 6 | — | 1 | 7 |
| Gurav | 3 | — | 2 | 5 |
| Kachi | 1 | — | 1 | 2 |
| Kahar | 1 | — | — | 1 |
| Kanoujia, parit, dhobi | 14 | 1 | 5 | 20 |
| Khalwar | — | — | 1 | 1 |
| Khangar | 1 | — | — | 1 |
| Koli | 1 | — | 1 | 2 |
| Kori | 1 | — | — | 1 |
| Mahli | — | — | 1 | 1 |
| Nai, nhari | 3 | 5 | 11 | 19 |
| Pardesi | 3 | 1 | 2 | 6 |
| Pasi | 1 | — | — | 1 |
| Tamboli | — | — | 1 | 1 |
| Total | 51 | 22 | 68 | 141 |
| | | | | |
| *Mahar* | 41 | 9 | 80 | 130 |
| *Other Scheduled Castes* | | | | |
| Bhangi | — | 1 | — | 1 |
| Burud | 1 | — | — | 1 |
| Chamar, chambhar | 3 | 5 | 5 | 13 |
| Dumar | 3 | — | — | 3 |
| Ghasi | 1 | — | — | 1 |
| Gowari | 7 | 1 | 9 | 17 |
| Katia | 1 | — | — | 1 |
| Khatik | 2 | 4 | 1 | 7 |

| CASTE GROUPS | NUMBER OF COUPLES | | | |
| --- | --- | --- | --- | --- |
| | City | Towns | Villages | Total |
| *Other Scheduled Castes (continued)* | | | | |
| Mang | 3 | — | 1 | 4 |
| Matang | 2 | — | 1 | 3 |
| Mehtar | 7 | 2 | — | 9 |
| Mochi | 3 | 1 | 4 | 8 |
| Total | 33 | 14 | 21 | 68 |
| *Gond* | 13 | — | 37 | 50 |
| *Other Castes* | | | | |
| Adivasi | 1 | — | — | 1 |
| Gosai | — | — | 2 | 2 |
| Goswami | — | 1 | — | 1 |
| Kalar | 24 | 1 | 11 | 36 |
| Kayastha | 8 | — | — | 8 |
| Kshatriya | 1 | 1 | 5 | 7 |
| Lingayat | 2 | 6 | 3 | 11 |
| Lodhi | — | 1 | 2 | 3 |
| Meroo Kshatriya | 4 | — | — | 4 |
| Nath | — | — | 3 | 3 |
| Pardeshi | 8 | — | — | 8 |
| Rajput | 2 | — | 12 | 14 |
| Telanga | 4 | 1 | — | 5 |
| Telegu | 12 | — | — | 12 |
| Thakur | 4 | — | 5 | 9 |
| Vaid | — | — | 1 | 1 |
| Other | 32 | 1 | 10 | 43 |
| Total | 102 | 12 | 54 | 168 |
| *Grand Total* | 882 | 309 | 1123 | 2314 |

# Appendix 2

## The Classification of Occupations

THE method of occupational classification employed in this study is based on the procedure developed by the Gokhale Institute of Politics and Economics, Poona, in its *Social Survey of Kolhapur City*, 1952. The institute noted the specific occupational status of each adult male and then grouped them into fourteen classes. Three of these classes—pensioners, beggars, and unemployed—pertain to non-earners. The eleven classes for earners are not purely "skill" or purely "status" grades but rather "skill-status" grades. The institute numbers and titles the classes in the following manner:

1) Unskilled Manual Work
2) Skilled Manual Work
3) Lower Professions and Administrative Posts, Primary Teachers
4) Small Businesses
5) Highly Skilled and Supervisory Manual Work
6) Clerks and Shop-Assistants
7) Intermediate Professions and Salaried Posts, Secondary Teachers
8) Medium Business
9) High Professions and Administrative Posts
10) Owners of Factories, Large Shops, etc.
11) Pensioners
12) Beggars, Prostitutes
13) Unemployed
14) Agriculturalists

In adopting this classificatory scheme, we have reduced the number of groups from fourteen to seven, using a method suggested by the Institute. We have combined classes 1 and 12 (Unskilled), 2 and 5 (Artisan), 3 and 6 (Clerical), 4, 8, and 10 (Trade), and 7 and 9 (Professional and Administrative). The last group also includes primary teachers but the other lower professions are combined with the clerks. Lastly, pensioners and other retired persons are grouped according to their main occupation prior to retirement.

| | NUMBER OF HUSBANDS | | | |
| OCCUPATIONAL GROUPS | City | Towns | Villages | Total |
| --- | --- | --- | --- | --- |
| *Unskilled* | | | | |
| Agricultural tenant or laborer | 5 | 7 | 99 | 111 |
| Coolie | 10 | — | 10 | 20 |
| Railroad worker, construction worker, etc. | 20 | 13 | 32 | 65 |
| Servant | 15 | 7 | 17 | 39 |
| Shepherd | — | — | 4 | 4 |
| Sweeper | 14 | 3 | 1 | 18 |
| Watchman | 9 | 2 | 4 | 15 |
| Total | 73 | 32 | 167 | 272 |
| *Artisans* | | | | |
| Skilled | | | | |
| Barber | 5 | 5 | 12 | 22 |
| Basket maker or drum maker | 4 | 3 | 1 | 8 |
| Blacksmith | 3 | 3 | 5 | 11 |
| Butcher | 1 | 3 | — | 4 |
| Carpenter | 12 | 7 | 29 | 48 |
| Cobbler or leather worker | 4 | 6 | 8 | 18 |
| Cook | 6 | — | 1 | 7 |
| Driver (cart, rickshaw, etc.) | 14 | 1 | 15 | 30 |
| Factory worker | 82 | 1 | 27 | 110 |
| Fisherman | 2 | 6 | 7 | 15 |
| Gardener | 1 | 3 | 4 | 8 |
| Mason | 3 | 1 | 2 | 6 |
| Painter | 1 | — | — | 1 |
| Potter | — | 2 | 5 | 7 |

## CLASSIFICATION OF OCCUPATIONS

| OCCUPATIONAL GROUPS | NUMBER OF HUSBANDS | | | |
| --- | --- | --- | --- | --- |
| | City | Towns | Villages | Total |
| *Artisans* (*continued*) | | | | |
| Washerman | 12 | — | 1 | 13 |
| Weaver | 39 | 36 | 75 | 150 |
| Highly Skilled | | | | |
| Electrician | 4 | — | — | 4 |
| Fitter (railroad) | 6 | — | 2 | 8 |
| Foreman | 5 | 2 | 2 | 9 |
| Goldsmith or jeweler | 15 | 5 | 3 | 23 |
| Jobber | 1 | — | — | 1 |
| Mechanic | 7 | 1 | 5 | 13 |
| Motor driver | 5 | — | 6 | 11 |
| Press worker | 8 | — | 2 | 10 |
| Sculpture | 3 | — | 3 | 6 |
| Tailor | 40 | 11 | 31 | 82 |
| Telegrapher | 2 | — | — | 2 |
| Welder | 2 | — | — | 2 |
| Total | 287 | 96 | 246 | 629 |
| *Trade* | | | | |
| Small Business | | | | |
| Bangle seller | 1 | — | 1 | 2 |
| Cart lender | 1 | — | 2 | 3 |
| Fruit or vegetable seller | 18 | 10 | 7 | 35 |
| Fuel dealer | 7 | — | 5 | 12 |
| Grass seller | — | — | 3 | 3 |
| Milk dealer | 10 | — | 12 | 22 |
| Mutton seller | 2 | — | — | 2 |
| Panthela owner, bidi seller, etc. | 14 | 1 | 6 | 21 |
| Large Business | | | | |
| Bicycle shop owner | 7 | — | 1 | 8 |
| Broker | 2 | — | — | 2 |
| Building Contractor | 4 | — | 3 | 7 |
| Business agent | 6 | 2 | 1 | 9 |

*Trade* (*continued*)

| OCCUPATIONAL GROUPS | NUMBER OF HUSBANDS | | | |
| --- | --- | --- | --- | --- |
| | City | Towns | Villages | Total |
| Cinema owner | 3 | — | — | 3 |
| Cloth merchant | 3 | 4 | 2 | 9 |
| Film distributor | 2 | — | — | 2 |
| Grain merchant | 4 | 2 | 9 | 15 |
| Grocery store owner | 17 | 9 | 10 | 36 |
| Hotel owner | 4 | 5 | 4 | 13 |
| Landlord | 6 | 2 | 5 | 13 |
| Machine shop owner | 1 | — | — | 1 |
| Sweet meat shop | 6 | — | — | 6 |
| Miscellaneous businesses | 67 | 6 | 29 | 102 |
| Total | 185 | 41 | 100 | 326 |

*Clerical*

Lower Professions and
Admin. Posts

| | City | Towns | Villages | Total |
| --- | --- | --- | --- | --- |
| Ayurvedic or homeo-<br>pathic doctor | 5 | 3 | 4 | 12 |
| Band master or musician | 2 | — | — | 2 |
| Bus conductor | 2 | — | — | 2 |
| Compounder | 2 | — | 1 | 3 |
| Constable or soldier | 4 | — | 6 | 10 |
| Mission worker, priest, etc. | 2 | — | 3 | 5 |
| Peon | 23 | 7 | 6 | 36 |
| Postman | 3 | — | 1 | 4 |

Clerks

| | City | Towns | Villages | Total |
| --- | --- | --- | --- | --- |
| Business clerk or<br>stenographer | 9 | — | — | 9 |
| Government clerk,<br>cashier etc. | 88 | 5 | 9 | 102 |
| Process writer | 1 | — | — | 1 |
| Shop assistant | 9 | — | — | 9 |
| Timekeeper | 2 | — | 1 | 3 |
| Total | 152 | 15 | 31 | 198 |

# CLASSIFICATION OF OCCUPATIONS

| OCCUPATIONAL GROUPS | NUMBER OF HUSBANDS | | | |
| --- | --- | --- | --- | --- |
| | City | Towns | Villages | Total |
| *Professional and Administrative* | | | | |
| Middle Prof. and Admin. | | | | |
| Accountant, auditor, patwari, etc. | 14 | 5 | 10 | 29 |
| Business manager | 15 | — | 1 | 16 |
| Engineer | 4 | — | 1 | 5 |
| Government or railway inspector | 8 | — | 1 | 9 |
| Office manager, overseer, etc. | 16 | — | 2 | 18 |
| Police inspector, kotwal, etc. | 3 | 4 | 18 | 25 |
| Railway conductor | 8 | — | 1 | 9 |
| Reporter | 1 | — | — | 1 |
| Social worker, development officer, etc. | 5 | — | 8 | 13 |
| Teacher | 33 | 14 | 27 | 74 |
| Higher Prof. and Admin. | | | | |
| Advocate, pleader | 5 | — | — | 5 |
| Banker | 1 | — | — | 1 |
| Doctor (M.B.B.S.) | 7 | — | 1 | 8 |
| Editor, publisher | 2 | — | — | 2 |
| Executive officer, patel, etc. | 14 | 1 | 12 | 27 |
| Labour leader | 1 | — | — | 1 |
| Professor | 6 | — | — | 6 |
| Total | 143 | 24 | 82 | 249 |
| *Agricultural* | | | | |
| Cultivator | 21 | 94 | 439 | 554 |
| Dairy farmer | 2 | 5 | 50 | 57 |
| Total | 23 | 99 | 489 | 611 |
| *Unemployed* | 19 | 2 | 8 | 29 |
| Grand Total | 882 | 309 | 1123 | 2314 |

143

# Appendix 3
## References Cited

Agarwala, S. N. "The Age at Marriage in India," *Population Index*, April 1957, pp. 96–107.

Census of India, 1951. Madhya Pradesh. *Nagpur District Census Handbook* by J. D. Kerawalla, Nagpur: Government Printing, Madhya Pradesh, 1952.

Census of India, 1951. Part I-A, *Report*. Delhi: Manager of Publications, 1953.

Chandrasekharan, C. "India's Population Problem," Unpublished Paper presented at the Inaugural Conference of the Demographic Teaching and Research Centre, Bombay, November 5, 1957.

Coale, Ansley J., and Edgar M. Hoover. *Population Growth and Economic Development in Low-Income Countries*. Princeton: Princeton University Press, 1958.

Dandekar, V. M., and K. Dandekar. *Survey of Fertility of Mortality in Poona District*. Poona: Gokhale Institute of Politics and Economics, Publication No. 27, 1953.

Davis, Kingsley. *The Population of India and Pakistan*. Princeton: Princeton University Press, 1951.

*Demographic Yearbook*, 1960. New York: United Nations, 1960.

Desai, I. P. "The Joint Family in India—An Analysis," *Sociological Bulletin*, V (September 1956), pp. 144–156.

Dube, S. C. *Indian Village*. London: Routledge and Kegan Paul, Ltd., 1955.

Ghurye, G. S. *Caste and Class in India*. Third Edition. Bombay: Popular Book Depot, 1957.

Government of India, Planning Commission. *Second Five-Year Plan*. Delhi: Manager of Publications, 1956.

Government of India, Planning Commission. *The New India: Progress Through Democracy*. New York: Macmillan, 1958.

144

Gupta, A. D., R. K. Sen, M. Majumdar, and S. N. Mitra. *The National Sample Survey, No. 7: Couple Fertility.* New Delhi: Department of Economic Affairs, Ministry of Finance: Government of India, 1955.

Hutton, J. H. *Caste in India.* Second Edition. Bombay: Oxford University Press, 1951.

Jain, S. P. *Relationship between Fertility and Economic and Social Status in the Punjab.* Lahore: Punjab Board of Economic Inquiry, Publication No. 64, 1939.

Jhabvala, R. P. *The Householder.* New York: Norton, 1960.

Kapadia, K. M. "Changing Patterns of Hindu Marriage and Family, [Part] III," *Sociological Bulletin,* IV (September 1955), pp. 161–192.

Kapadia, K. M. *Marriage and Family in India.* Second Edition. Bombay: Oxford University Press, 1958.

Kapadia, K. M. "Rural Family Patterns," Sociological Bulletin, V (September 1956), pp. 111–126.

Markadanaya, Kamala. *Nectar in the Sieve.* New York: New American Library, 1956.

Nagpur Improvement Trust. *Master Plan of Nagpur 1953.* Nagpur: Government Printing, Madhya Pradesh, 1954.

Opler, Marvin K. "Family, Anxiety, and Religion in a Community of North India," *Culture and Mental Health,* edited by Marvin K. Opler. New York: Macmillan, 1959, pp. 273–289.

Poti, S. J., and S. Dutta. "Social Mobility and Differential Fertility," Unpublished Paper presented at the Third All India Sociological Conference, Agra, February 1958.

Ross, Aileen. *The Hindu Family in Its Urban Setting.* Toronto: University of Toronto Press, 1961.

Sovani, N. V., and K. Dandekar. *Fertility Survey of Nasik, Kolaba, and Satara (North) Districts.* Poona: Gokhale Institute of Politics and Economics, Publication No. 31, 1955.

Sovani, N. V. *The Social Survey of Kolhapur City, Part I—Population and Fertility.* Poona: The Gokhale Institute of Politics and Economics, Publication No. 18, 1948.

"Symposium: Caste and Joint Family," *Sociological Bulletin,* IV (September 1955), pp. 83–146.

United Nations, Bureau of Social Affairs. *International Survey of Programmes of Social Development.* New York: United Nations, 1959.

World Health Organization. *Final Report on Pilot Studies in Family Planning.* New Delhi, 1954.

Zinkin, Taya. *India Changes.* New York: Oxford University Press, 1958.

# Index 🐚

abortion, 114, 115, 116
Agarwala, S. N., 57
age, 17
    of husbands, 61
    of wives and:
        birth control, 114, 115, 116;
        caste, 47-48, 65; child mortali-
        ty, 104, 106; education, 54-55,
        71; employment status, 50, 67;
        family structure, 41-43, 45ff;
        fertility, 9, 13, 73-75, 78ff;
        ideal number of children, 120;
        income, 51, 69; interest in
        family limitation, 119; land
        ownership, 52, 69; marital sta-
        tus, 12, 78-79, 132; number of
        living children, 106; occupa-
        tion, 49, 66; religion, 45-46, 63;
        residence, 44, 62
    *see also* age at marriage
age at marriage, 33, Ch. 4; caste
    and, 63-65, 72, 91; education and,
    70-72, 100; employment status
    and, 66-68; estimation of, 17; fer-
    tility and, 12, 13, 14, 57, 58, 72,
    83ff; husband-wife difference in,
    59ff; for husbands, 59ff; income
    and, 67-69, 72, 96, 97; land own-
    ership and, 68-69, 97, 98; by law,
    59, 60; occupation and, 65-66, 72,
    93, 94; in Poona District, 58; re-
    ligion and, 62-63, 72, 88; resi-
    dence and, 58, 61-62, 86, 87;
    studies of, 57-58; trends in, 57-
    58, 60, 72; in Union of India, 57-
    58; of wives, 58-72, 86, 87, 88, 91,
    93, 94, 96, 97, 98, 100
agricultural production, 3
Aiyappan, A., 38
authority, 34-35

Bihar, 3
biology, effect on fertility, 76, 127
birth, 4, 8
birth control, 16, 17, 73, Ch. 7;
    natural, 127; programs, 5; tech-
    niques: 114-115, 130, 133; age
    and, 114; caste and, 122-123; edu-
    cation and, 125-126; employment
    status and, 123-124; income and,

124; interest in family limitation
and, 117-118; land ownership and,
125; occupation and, 123; opposition to, 117, 127-128; popularity
of, 130; religion and, 121-122;
residence and, 121; use of, 80-81,
115-117, 130
*see also* family limitation
birth place, 31-32
births, spacing of, 76; *see also* fer-
    tility
Bombay University, 37

Calcutta, 59
caste, 7, 15; age at marriage and,
    63-65, 72, 91; age of wife and,
    47-48, 65; birth control and, 122-
    123; child mortality and, 107-
    108; family structure and, 37, 38,
    45-48, 55; fertility and, 8, 10, 11,
    13, 85, 88-92, 108, 132, 135; in-
    terest in family limitation and,
    122-123; number of living chil-
    dren and, 108; residence and,
    135-138
castes, classification of, Appendix 1
castes, list of: Adivasi, 138; Agar-
    wal, 135; Ahir, 136; Badai, 136;
    Badhi, 136; Bania, 46-48, 64-65,
    89-92, 108, 122, 136; Baria, 137;
    Barhai, 136; Beldar, 137; Bhangi,
    137; Bhoi, 137; Brahmin, 8, 12,
    32-33, 46-48, 55, 63-65, 72, 89-
    92, 107-108, 122-123, 135; Burad,
    137; Burud, 137; Chamar, 137;
    Chambhar, 137; Chatri, 136;
    Chhatri, 135; Darzi, 136; Dhangar,
    137; Dhimar, 137; Dhobi, 46-47;
    64-65, 89-92, 108, 122, 137; Du-
    mar, 137; Gaoli, 19, 137; Ghasi,
    137; Gond, 46-47, 64-65, 89-92,
    108, 122-123, 135, 138; Gosai, 138;
    Goswami, 138; Gowari, 137; Gu-
    jerati, 135; Gurav, 137; Halwai,
    135; Jaiswal, 135; Javeri, 135;
    Kachi, 137; Kachwadi, 136; Ka-
    har, 137; Kalar, 138; Kanoujia,
    137; Kasar, 136; Katia, 137;
    Kayastha, 138; Khachwadi, 136;
    Khalwar, 137; Khangar, 137;

National Sample Survey, *see* Government of India
natural increase, 3
nuptial room, 39

occupation, and: age, 49, 66; age at marriage, 65-66, 72, 93-94; birth control, 123; child mortality, 108-109; family structure, 34, 48-50, 56; fertility, 9, 13, 92-94, 102, 109, 132; interest in family limitation, 123, 130; number of living children, 109; residence, 140-143
occupational change, 6, 131
occupations, list of, Appendix 2
Office of Population Research, 4, 5
Opler, M. E., 12
Orissa, 3

parents, 128
Parsees, *see* religion
patriotism, 129
plague, 3
population growth, 3, 4, 5, 103, 112, 113, 117, 128, 129
postnatal care, 12, 132
Poti, S. J., 40
pregnancy, 11, 12, 13, 132; *see also* abortion
prestige, 128
property inheritance, 37, 129
puberty, 76; *see also* menstruation
Poona District, 7, 8, 10, 58
Punjab, 9

religion, 6, 7, 25, 26, 27, 32; age and, 45-46, 63; age at marriage and, 62-63, 72, 88; birth control and, 12, 117, 121-122, 132; change in, 131; child mortality and, 107; family structure and, 44-46, 55; fertility and, 8, 11, 13, 85, 87-88, 107, 127, 130, 132, 133; interest in family limitation and, 121-122, 127, 130; number of living children and, 107
remarriage, 25, 33, 77-80, 117, 127
reproduction, physiology of, 12, 58
reproductive rate, 8; *see also* fertility
residence, 6, 7, 26, 27, 32; age and, 44, 62; age at marriage and, 58, 61-62, 72, 86-87; birth control

and, 121; caste and, 135-138; change in, 131; child mortality and, 106-107; choice of, 36; family structure and, 37, 38, 39, 40, 43-44, 55; fertility and, 8, 10, 11, 13, 84-87, 102, 106-107; interest in family limitation and, 121, 130; number of living children and, 106-107; occupation and, 140-143
rhythm method, 114, 115, 116; *see also* birth control
Ross, A. D., 37, 45
rural area, *see* residence

sample, adequacy of, 15, 25-33; random, 25-26; size and selection of, 18-25
sanitation programs, 113
Satara District, 8
Saurashtra, 38, 55
self control, 114; *see also* social control
Sen, R. K., 8, 58
sexual abstinence, 12, 40, 82, 113, 115, 116, 117, 132
sexual intercourse, 12, 39, 55, 114, 132
Sikhs, *see* religion
smallpox, 3
social change, 131
social control, 39, 55, 129
social development, 3
social norms, 5
social mobility, 40
social objectives, 3
social organization, 34
social power, 128
social prestige, 34, 40
social security, 34
social status, 7, 23, 37
social structure, 5, 7, 131, 132
social values, 36
sons, preference for, 129
Sovani, N. V., 8, 9, 10
spinsters, 10, 132
standard of living, 129
states, reorganization of, 18
sterility, 3, 11, 75, 117, 132; *see also* fertility
sterilization, 114, 115, 116, 117, 129
subordination, *see* authority

151